EVERYTHING YOU NEED TO KNOW

MOTORCYCLE TOURING

DR. GREGORY W. FRAZIER

motorbooks

First published in 2005 by MBI Publishing
Company and Motorbooks, an imprint of MBI
Publishing Company, 400 1st Avenue North, Suite
300, Minneapolis, MN 55401 USA

Motorbooks titles are also available at discounts in
bulk quantity for industrial or sales-promotional
use. For details write to Special Sales Manager at
MBI Publishing Company, 400 1st Avenue North,
Suite 300, Minneapolis, MN 55401 USA.

To find out more about our books, join us online at
www.motorbooks.com.

ISBN-13: 978-0-7603-2035-8

Editor: Peter Schletty
Designer: Brenda C. Canales
Printed in China

On the front cover: *Photo by Kevin Wing*

On the frontispiece: Gorgeous vistas like this ocean
view are the rewards of a long trip on two wheels.

On the back cover: *(left)* The cockpit of the
motorcycle tourer. You may not need all of
these luxuries. Or maybe you'll need more.
The point is for you to know your travel style and
to be prepared.
(right) Spending your nights in a tent can make
motorcycle touring more affordable. Whether
you stay in a designated public or private
campsite, or simply claim a patch of grass for the
night, you're carrying your shelter wherever the
road takes you.

CONTENTS

About the Author

Professional motorcycle adventurer Dr. Gregory W. Frazier is the only motorcyclist in the world to have four times circumnavigated the globe solo by motorcycle. No stranger to danger, his adventures around the earth include having been shot at by rebels, jailed by unfriendly authorities, bitten by snakes, run over by Pamplona bulls, and smitten by a product of Adam's rib.

Frazier's two wheel travels have taken him over 1,000,000 miles and he has literally "ridden a motorcycle to the ends of the earth": Dead Horse, Alaska; Ushuaia, Argentina; North Cape, Norway; Cape Agulhaus, South Africa; and Bluff, New Zealand.

Frazier's work as a motorcycle journalist and photographer appears widely throughout the international motorcycling press. He is a regular columnist for *Road Bike* and *Dual Sport News* and contributes to *Rider, Motorcycle Consumer News, Motorcyclist,* and *American Motorcyclist* in the United States. Internationally, his work has appeared in *BMW Bikes* (Japan), *Tourenfahrer* (Germany), *Motorrad* (Germany) and *Motorcycle Trader and News* (New Zealand). He has been featured in other foreign publications such as *Motor*

Cycle News (Great Britain) and *Moto* (Russia). Known for his travel articles, he also enjoys a solid reputation for motorcycle and product evaluations.

As a documentary film producer, Frazier has made numerous contributions to the film industry and motorcycling history with films such as *Vintage Iron, Mexico by Motorcycle, Motorcycling on the Ten Best Highways in America, Motorcycling on the Ten Best Highways in the Alps, Motorcycling to Alaska* and *Motorcycling Down Under (Australia and New Zealand).* A recent release, *Two Wheel Wanderlust: Traveling Around the World By Motorcycle,* is a video documentary of motorcycle adventurers who have roamed the globe from 1913 to 2000.

Dr. Frazier is also an accomplished motorcycle racer, having won races with BMW and Indian motorcycles. His name can be found in the Pikes Peak Race Course record books aboard both marques, and road race tracks throughout the United States and Canada have seen him as a successful competitor on a wide variety of race bikes including Honda and Yamaha. As the founder of the BMW G/S Big Dog Ride and the Elephant Ride he has enjoyed both events as organizer and entrant. Frazier is also a well-known motivational speaker, often times presenting his multi-media show *Sun Chasing: Four Times Around The World By Motorcycle*.

In August 2002, Frazier completed his fourth solo motorcycle circumnavigation of the globe, becoming the first motorcyclist in the world to have accomplished such a feat. His 2002 effort included crossing all eight time zones of Russia. In 2004 Frazier started his fifth motorcycle ride around the earth, helping a Parkinson's patient "Ride The Dream." The website www.ultimategloberide.com follows their adventure as they circle the globe.

When not adventuring around the world, Frazier, a Crow Indian ("Sun Chaser"), lives in the Big Horn Mountains of Montana on the Crow Indian Reservation. He says of his adventures, "*I hate adventure that has anything to do with snakes or sharks.*"

Books published include:

Alaska By Motorcycle, Riding the World, Europe by Motorcycle, New Zealand by Motorcycle, Riding South: Mexico, Central America, and South America by Motorcycle, Motorcycle Sex: Freud Would Never Understand the Relationship Between Me and My Motorcycle, Motorcycle Poems By the Biker Poet, Motorcycle Cemetery Tales, Indian Motorcycles International Directory, and *BMW GSing Around the World*

Motodromomania: An extreme form of a psychological disorder associated with motorcycle touring, also known as two-wheel vagabond neurosis. It is classified in the category of impulse control disorders. Those diagnosed with this disorder have an abnormal impulse to travel by motorcycle; they often spend beyond their means, and sacrifice lovers, jobs, and security in their lust for new two-wheel touring experiences. Motodromomaniacs feel more alive when traveling and no sooner return from a tour than they start planning their next tour. Much of their waking thoughts are spent fantasizing and talking about motorcycle touring, and often their nocturnal dreams are filled.

TOURING BY MOTORCYCLE:
101 TO ADVANCED

American Carl Sterns Clancy had completed the first 'round-the-world ride in 1913 and numerous cross-country motorcycle speed records had been set in America by the mid-1960s.

TOURING 101

Hookers and virgins. It was a Friday night and my first day of motorcycle touring had landed me in jail. I was a virgin motorcycle tourer locked up with a house full of unhappy prostitutes.

Motorcycle touring had been going on for 60 to 70 years by the time I became involved. American Carl Sterns Clancy had completed the first 'round-the-world ride in 1913 and numerous cross-country motorcycle speed records had been set in America by the mid-1960s.

All of this was unknown to me, a newbie on a Honda 305-cc Super Hawk at the time. I had read no books on motorcycle touring; in fact, I didn't know any existed. I had done some long day rides, but never any long-distance riding or touring.

College was letting out for the summer, and I was faced with several options in getting from Indiana back to Montana, the cheapest of which was to ride my motorcycle. Word got around and soon I was asked by someone more inexperienced than I (he had only been on the back of my motorcycle once before) if he could ride on the back to Minnesota, pooling our limited funds and sharing expenses. We made a plan to ride to Minneapolis where I would drop him off, then I would ride on solo to Montana.

I had done enough riding to know that wearing a helmet with a face shield was better than eating bugs, and safer than no helmet if we crashed, so we agreed to wear helmets. Leather jackets were next, something to ward off the rain, wind, and cold, or so we thought. But the best we could afford were a couple of used leather jackets, mine being suede with sheepskin lining, and my riding pal's a used bomber jacket from the local Army surplus store.

Gloves were the garden variety, but leather. Pants were jeans and boots were

My Honda 305-cc Super Hawk would outrun most anything my riding buddies had, and it never broke down. While my friends on their British motorcycles were afraid to take them farther than 10 or 20 miles from the college campus, and seldom rode at night, I could see no limits for the Honda.

leather cowboy boots for me and a set of Army boots for my buddy.

Next, we outfitted the motorcycle. I scratched and scrimped enough money to purchase a windscreen. Then we needed something to carry our clothes in the form

It was a Friday night and my first day of motorcycle touring had landed me in jail.

of saddlebags. Leather was expensive and voted out because all we could find was the pricey Harley-Davidson gear, and those were far too big for the Honda. Instead, we went back to the surplus store and bought a pair of small canvas carrying sacks that we tied to the rear of the bike. Once filled, they held about a quarter of what we deemed necessary for the ride home.

There was no rear luggage rack and the purchase price of anything that approximated one was beyond our limited budget. After a week of thinking, we finally settled on a sissy bar, the tallest we could find. With hose clamps and U-bolts we attached it to the subframe and started to tie things to it. On the front we tied two sleeping bags, and then to the back we attached a leather suitcase and a box of cooking equipment. This was in an era when the words *bungee cord*

were yet unknown, so to attach items to the motorcycle we used cheap clothesline cord purchased at the hardware store.

Once we got everything lashed to the Honda it looked manageable. No thought was given to a test ride. Instead, on the morning school finished for the summer, we suited up. I got on the overloaded Honda, then my riding buddy slipped and stuffed himself between me and the sissy bar, much like jamming a foot into a new shoe with a shoe horn. It was a tight fit, so tight that I was pushed far enough forward onto the gas tank that I spoke in soprano.

These friends are making an agreement on how to take a long ride together. The choice of whether to ride alone or together, on one bike or two, is a critical decision involving money, compatibility, and riding styles. I have tried all ways, and have found I am personally best when I ride solo. I trust myself more than I trust those riding around me, and I prefer the responsibility of taking care of my own equipment and myself to company. (See Chapter 1)

I eventually moved to an Indian Chief from the Honda. With four times the engine displacement, I felt I would have enough power to more comfortably carry a passenger as well as more gear. While I missed the electric starter on my Honda, I offset that with the rumbling sound of the big 1,200-cc engines of the Indians.

The Alpine riding in Europe is described as some of the best motorcycle riding in the world. In the summer, European motorcyclists swarm these roads. The motorcycles become the Kings of the Road, with cars and buses pulling over and allowing them to pass. To me it seemed like Motorcycling Heaven.

As we wobbled off the college campus and onto the main highway I never doubted we would succeed in reaching our goals of Minneapolis and Montana. The light rain that was coming down did not phase me, because I believed the new windscreen I was hunched behind would keep me dry.

Twenty miles later, soaked and wearing water-filled boots, we stopped at a department store and decided to spend some of our combined limited funds on two plastic rain suits. After struggling into them we wedged ourselves back onto the Honda and again wobbled onto the main highway. Less than 100 miles later I had to stop for gas

and warmth. As we stood dripping in the gas station parking lot, squeezing water from our gloves, jackets, and shirts, we realized the wind had shredded our new rain suits, literally blown them apart at the seams. Rather than spend more of our precious gas and food money, we decided not to replace them and ride on in hopes that the rain would stop and the sun would return to dry us out.

The day did get better after a stop for soup and warmth 50 miles later. We must have looked like guppies out of the fish bowl as we sloshed into the restaurant, but since it was a greasy truck stop with vinyl booths the only comment made was by the waitress: "Looks like you boys won't need a bath tonight."

Back on the highway with a stomach full of saltine crackers, catsup, and soup, the trip started to look better. The rain had stopped and I could drive closer to the speed limit, now being able to see through the plastic bubble shield that was not fogged on the inside and covered in rain splatters on the outside. I was nearly to the point of singing when the motorcycle started to run on only one of the two cylinders. We sputtered to a stop and I saw a cloud of oil behind us. The overworked Honda had holed a piston.

Looking back on that day I should have expected mechanical disaster sooner, much sooner. The 305-cc twin-cylinder motorcycle was fine for running around town, doing afternoon rides with a passenger on the back, but not suited for the way we were flogging it. It was so overburdened that the headlight lit the middle of the back end of semi-truck trailers. If I did not slip the clutch when starting from a dead stop, the front wheel would come off the ground.

By the time we were sidelined, the clutch was slipping when I gave the engine the slightest increase in gas. I naively assumed I could live with that, but the spewing oil and one running lung brought our tour to a halt.

We managed to push the motorcycle to a nearby gas station, from where we called the nearest Honda motorcycle shop. They told us if we could get it there by morning they might be able to fix us up and get us back on the road in the afternoon. With the help of a friendly pick-up driver we got ourselves into town and off-loaded at the motorcycle shop just before closing. The mechanic made a quick estimate of the financial damage, then pointed out how we were also in need of new clutch plates ("You'll never make it out of town.") and a new rear tire. ("Good luck finding one on Sunday. By the way, boys, either one of you know how to change a tire? Got any tools?")

The two of us road guppies gulped when we saw the estimate. Leaving the shop we knew the total of our pooled funds for food, gas, rooms, and fun were going to barely meet the cost of repairs. Instead of a nice warm room for the night we were faced with sleeping in wet sleeping bags, somewhere. We decided on City Park.

As we were setting up camp in City Park, the local police cruiser stopped and told us we could not sleep there. Dumbfounded, we told the policeman we had no money and did not know where we could sleep. After explaining our bike and money problems, my riding partner suggested, "Maybe we could sleep in your jail?"

The officer said, "Nope, we're not a flophouse and you guys would have to be arrested to spend the night there."

I have never checked, but I suspect we were arrested for vagrancy. We did some paperwork, had to give up all of our camping gear, pocket items, and me my belt and my buddy his boot laces. I do remember the booking sergeant told us,

"We don't want you boys hanging yourselves in there. It's Friday night, and if we get busy we might have to kick you boys out if we fill up." That's always made me think we were "kind of" booked, but not really.

Jail was no fun. Since we were maybe there and maybe not, they did not serve us any food. We were locked in a cell with two steel beds (no mattresses) hung from the wall, and a stainless steel commode and wash basin.

It was Friday night and the local constables were busy busting prostitutes. By 10 p.m. the cells around us were filled with some of the wildest women my Quaker college pal and I had ever imagined, and the

One of the survival skills I've learned is that the world deals with motorcycle maintenance differently than I was taught in the United States. Here, in India, is how a motorcyclist replaces a worn tire by having it recapped. You take the old tire to a tire repairman who melts on a new outer layer and grooves it. As the average speed limit on the roads seldom exceeded 35 miles per hour, this is often an adequate fix for the budget-minded traveler.

Here I met two motorcyclists touring Asia. The man on the left was from the Netherlands and had spent a year in India collecting enough parts to hand-build his touring motorcycle. The other man purchased his "as is," which included leaking fork seals that made his front brake unusable. Neither was daunted by the state of their equipment and had several months of touring planned.

What was once the world's largest motorcycle, the Brazilian made Amazonas first started out as a Volkswagen engine stuffed into an Indian motorcycle frame. The company was later sold and went into full production from the ground up. The Amazonas came with a reverse gear; the transmission and engine coming from the Volkswagen factory in Brazil. Less than 1,000 were produced, but they were a favorite with the motorcycle police of Brazil because they would not overheat like the Harley-Davidsons did. This was due to a Volkswagen fan used for cooling the engine.

ladies were having a great time making fun of us. We were offered everything we could translate from their gutter English, and what we could not understand we were shown. By midnight the jailhouse had become a party house, and the two motorcycle babies (someone had ratted us out) were the center of the party, the butt of every joke, and any reason to bare breasts and other unmentionables to see if we were awake and get our blood flowing to our faces. By morning, with no sleep, both of us wished the jail had

become so crowded that we had been kicked out.

Back at the Honda shop when they opened, we sat on the sidewalk while the mechanic labored on until late afternoon when we finally got the bill and the bike.

What was left of our money got us to Minneapolis, where my buddy unloaded himself and his share of the luggage, then waited for his parents to pick him up. We had eaten nothing for two days, but the bike ran better than before and our miles per gallon had gone to nearly twice what it was before. His parents lent me $20 and I started off across the Dakotas toward home.

With the weight cut by half, my Honda and I flew. I was so worried about more bad weather and mechanical breakdowns I decided to ride through the night. Watching my cash dwindle as the sun set, I knew I could not afford a motel or food. Rough calculations told me I would run out of money and gas before I landed at my parent's house.

That night I began thinking outside the box for motorcycle touring. The gas stations would turn off the electric power to the pumps when they closed, but this was the Dakotas and people were more trustworthy than today, so the nozzles were not padlocked to the pumps. I would ride into a closed gas station, unhook the nozzles, and then hold the hose high in the air, draining out what gas was left in the hose in to my gas tank. In a small town with several gas stations I managed twice during the night to top off my gas tank.

About 100 miles from home, I was out of gas, cash, and luck. I had ridden into several gas stations and asked to "borrow" enough gas to get me home. The responses from the gas station attendants ranged from, "If you want to borrow something, try the bank," to, "Huh?"

My gas tank on reserve, I left town. As I passed over a river I saw a boat down below tied to a dock with a 5-gallon red gas can connected to the motor and no one around. I turned around, scanned the area, then "borrowed" about 3 of the 5 gallons. I scribbled a note and left it on the gas can handle with my parent's telephone number and a promise to pay.

That 3 gallons got me home, and I never did receive a telephone call. I went back several times to try and find the owner but never could. The lesson I learned that day was the difference between two-stroke motors and four-stroke motors. As my Honda wheezed and smoked into the Honda motorcycle shop some days later for more expensive repairs, the mechanic asked me, "Hey, did you put two-stroke mix in this bike?"

That was the end of my first course in Motorcycle Touring, Class 101. I had not only learned about the difference between two-stroke and four-stroke engines, but I had also learned about weight, tires, riding gear, packing, mileage, pick-up trucks, and headlight adjustment. In addition, I had expanded my Quaker vocabulary to include some words I would be able to ably use in and out of context for the rest of my life, made some new friends, and learned things about women that likewise would be applicable the rest of my life. The bucketful of experiences on that first motorcycle tour of mid-America also taught me I had a 500-gallon barrel to fill, and it was fun filling it up.

ADVANCED MOTORCYCLE TOURING

Big motorcycles were one answer to my touring shortcomings, so I moved to 1,200-cc Indians and Harley-Davidsons. The guys who seemed to be doing the long riding for extended periods were on Harleys, and the Harley-Davidson dealer offered accessories such as windscreens, jackets, luggage racks, and saddlebags to make the trips easier. It was from the Harley riders I started to get advice on touring and how to overcome the mistakes I had made with the Honda.

The Indians and the Harleys began my "adventure" riding, if adventure riding is defined in the strictest sense. Webster's definition includes the word *risk*, which is quite appropriate in my case. With both brands there it was always the risk I would not make my destination and that mechanical problems would bring me up short. I soon learned how to become not only a rider but also a shade tree mechanic when the bikes died. Sometimes it was an adventure just to make it across town. Other times I knew my tour would include some down

time, so my toolkit started to grow, as did my mechanical skill. I can still remember looking at rusting cars and wire fences as possible supply points when I passed them. A monkey wrench, hammer, and a couple of screwdrivers always had a home in a saddlebag. I soon learned that the small tool boxes bolted to the fenders of Harleys and Indians were more for looks than carrying the tools needed for roadside repairs.

With the bigger bikes I was able to carry more gear comfortably, and when the bikes ran, they fed my hunger for roaming away from home. I added a tent, cook stove, and better weather gear like rubber irrigation ditch boots and spare tubes, an

With the bigger bikes I was able to carry more gear comfortably, and when the bikes ran, they fed my hunger for roaming away from home.

air pump, then a flashlight for when the beasts died at night.

The Japanese bikes at this time were starting to get bigger, moving into the 450-cc, then 750-cc range. But it was the BMWs that really hooked me on touring. I had seen some posters in the late 1960s with riders in

As I worked my way through Asia I found myself touring on a 500-cc Indian-made Enfield Bullet. It carried me four months into Nepal, Sikkum, Bangladesh, and back to India, for 10,000 kilometers. It disproved all my previous learning about English-made motorcycles by not having a single "Lucas" electrical problem during the entire ride. In fact, the only problem it did have was a broken throttle cable, a $1 part in India.

In parts of the world where "big bikes" are expensive due to high import taxes and are hard to find, I learned to change my road "lifestyle" for touring and adjust to smaller-displacement engines. One of the advantages to using the smaller motorcycles is the ability to get off the pavement and into more remote parts of the world. Here my Honda was taking me into the jungles near the border of Burma.

Africa and magazine articles about riding in the Alps. Their motorcycles had equipment I could not find at my local motorcycle shop. I often had to make do with what I could cobble together, like backpacks for saddlebags and, horror of horrors, a Harley-Davidson windshield affixed to the front of my new German R69US in 1969. When I rode into the local BMW shop for a tune up with the Harley windscreen the German mechanic muttered words I had never heard before and bemoaned the fact that the clamps had cracked the fine German chrome on the handlebars.

I had become obsessed with riding, and riding far away from home for as long as I could stay away. The BMW got me back and forth across the United States, into Mexico and Canada, and it always got me home. Some expensive German accessories had to be imported, like hand-molded aluminum handlebar fairings and leg protectors.

Then, tired of the lack of accessories and clothing, I made the big leap in 1970 and flew to Europe to take delivery on a new

BMW at the factory. The first stop after collecting the motorcycle was a leather motorcycle clothing store for everything from boots to helmets. The next stop was a motorcycle shop for some BMW after-market accessories like a German full fairing and English fiberglass saddlebags.

A month later, I had covered much of Europe. I saw that the Europeans were well ahead of Americans when it came to rider protection, raingear, and touring accessories. This time was probably not the most interesting for my then wife who was riding pillion. She wanted to stop and poke through castles, look into churches, and visit museums. On the other hand, I would vector into any motorcycle shop I saw, looking for motorcycle touring accessories and talking with other travelers about their equipment. From Spain to England, I can still feel her twisting to look at castles as we rode as fast as the BMW would run on autobahns bound for the next bike supply point, meeting, or shop.

When I returned to the United States, the fully equipped touring bike followed,

Two Kawasaki KLR owners agree that although their bikes have been outfitted differently to meet the different requirements of each rider, the Kawasaki was the favorite touring motorcycle for both of them.

and I spent my free time exploring America, less wet (thanks to European raingear), breaking down less often (sold the Harleys and parked the Indian), learning more about motorcycle maintenance (road racing and wrenching), and picking up survival skills by watching others and benefiting from some off-road riding. More trips into Mexico, Canada, then Alaska taught me to adjust to foreign driving habits, fill out necessary paperwork, and how best to eat and sleep on the road.

Technology and equipment was making touring more comfortable. A British motorcycle salesman was walking out of a motorcycle shop one day having failed at selling one or both of the two new Nortons in his van. He made me an offer that I politely refused, but then, like the guy selling watches on the streets of New York City, he said, "Well, if you don't need a bike, how about some of these?" and pulled out a clump of bungee cords. I bought every one he had and that was the last time I used rope on a motorcycle other than to pull one when it died or was broken.

The late 1970s produced more and more techno-touring equipment. Honda was the King of Gadgets for bikes. They began carrying CBs, radios, and full body-work that put the rider in a bubble. It was about this time I found my first motorcycle-touring book. Written by Ken Craven, the book *Ride It: The Complete Motorcycle Touring Book* (Haynes 1977), was full of handy tips and advice on touring by motorcycle. In the first chapter, Craven set the touring hook even deeper in my brain when he wrote, "If one has a motorcycle of any shape or size, providing it will hold together, well, you have a vehicle for conquering the globe and all you need now is the time and money. A motorcycle, large or small, is the superb unrivalled tool for providing more sheer joy per minute than anything else."

I had known what he was saying, but his saying it in 130 pages confirmed my youthful knowledge. From there I set out to conquer the globe. A first ride around the world proved to me that language and paperwork were not barriers but tests of wit and patience. Preparing the motorcycle and maintaining it while on a global tour gave a sense of satisfaction I could find in no other accomplishments in my life, and that included everything from education to catching fish.

A second and more difficult ride around the world, following a different route but in less time, proved how small the globe really is, being only about 24,000 miles around and most of that water.

A second ride around the world, proved how small the globe really is, being only about 24,000 miles around and most of that water.

Many of my "big bike" friends would scoff if they were told a 225-cc motorcycle was more than adequate for touring. I, however, adapted quite comfortably to this Yamaha TTR for use in Thailand, Cambodia, and Laos and toured for two or three months. I learned I could carry less and still enjoy touring. There was no room for gizmos and gadgets (see Chapter 8), but I was able to comfortably travel without them. What is surprising, however, is that I have seen on more than one occasion people touring two-up on one of these motorcycles.

A third ride around the world, using motorcycles indigenous to the continents I was crossing, required preparing and maintaining a mix of motorcycles that ranged from Amazonas in South America, to Indian and Harley-Davidson in North America, BMW in Europe, then Enfield, SYN, Hartford, and Honda across Asia. I carried my riding gear, tools and survival kit from continent to continent on airplanes, and modified each motorcycle to fit myself and riding conditions on the continent I was crossing.

A fourth ride around the world, done in five months on a new Kawasaki KLR 650, had me tagging borders I had not seen before, touring Russia across eight time zones, and testing modifications made to a motorcycle I was totally unfamiliar with from the sands of the Sahara to the cold rain and snow of the Alps.

On my long tours I would meet other travelers and we would compare equipment and touring styles. One of the first things I learned was what worked for me would often not work for others. I would choose aluminum panniers where the next tourer would be using large plastic camera cases. We would argue the merits of each and both would be equally satisfied that our personal choice was the best.

The same would be true for boots, helmets, riding suits, tires, windscreens, seats, tank bags, and, of course, choice of motorcycle. While one person would be blissfully happy sitting on a stock seat, another would swear that his or her $500 modified seat was superior. The person who paid $25,000 for a touring motorcycle and added $15,000 worth of accessories would gasp when I said I had never used a GPS, wondering how I had managed to make it from my home to a campground 200 miles away without getting lost.

With the advent of the digital world, computers, satellite telephones, laptop computers, CD players, digital cameras

Here I caught a couple of motorcyclists critically inspecting my touring bike. When they asked how many miles were on it they both developed more respect when I told them it had 142,000 miles and had been around the world.

and recorders, radios, and intercom systems became required touring equipment for many tourers. When I saw some of these fully loaded touring bikes with every electrical gizmo the owner could hang on it, and in some cases two or three (like GPSs) for back-up, I did not discount their choice of touring equipment. Instead, I would think back to the tour made by Sterns Clancy in 1912–1913, then about what Craven wrote about time and money.

Next month I will probably learn something new, a better skill or technique, discard the old.

All of us are seeing the world, traveling over it, around it, on it, by a two- or three-wheeled motorized cycle. We are moving through the environment of the earth, tasting and smelling it, not from the enclosed bubble of a car or bus or pressurized airplane. We are actually part of what we are passing through.

What follows are some things I have learned that have been helpful for me to manage riding over 1 million miles and four times around the earth. While I have not done it the fastest, longest, or hardest, I have managed to stay alive, mostly out of jail, and found some things that worked consistently for me.

Next month I will probably learn something new, a better skill or technique, discard the old, and smile knowing some more learning has been added to my 500-gallon barrel. I will submit to someone else claiming to have ridden more miles, his or her knowing more about mapping, computers, riding, and touring. At the same time, I will be the first to say that evening I spent in jail with my Quaker pal and the ladies of the night was where I learned a real truth to motorcycle touring, that being when the hooker next to us said, "Boys, you ain't seen nuthin' yet." But I seen some. Motorcycle touring, that is.

What follows are some things I have learned that have been helpful for me to manage riding over 1 million miles and four times around the earth.

ALONE OR TOGETHER

Chapter 1

Two of us started around the world in 2004 with a ride to the farthest point north on the North American continent we could reach, Deadhorse, Alaska. We chose the KLR because we knew we were going to be doing nearly 1,000 hard miles on gravel roads. My passenger, a 62-year-old grandmother of six, had Parkinson's disease and wanted to see the world from a motorcycle. The motorcycle was too small so we switched to larger, more comfortable motorcycles.

To tour alone or to travel with others is one of the first questions faced by the motorcyclist. Some prefer the independence of solo travel while others choose riding in a group, with their buddy, or sharing the experience with a spouse or significant other. Each option has ups and downs.

GOING SOLO

Independence is the primary advantage of traveling alone. You ride at your own pace, set your own clock, control your pit stops, and end each day when you're ready and have the freedom to make changes on a whim as you go. You are responsible to, and for, no one other than yourself.

There are numerous advantages to choosing the lone wolf travel style. These include reducing risk, limiting responsibility, and not having to share the experience. Additionally, there are other factors such as it being easier to find a place to stay at night, making more

acquaintances, and choosing a pace of travel that suits you.

When you invite or are asked to join others you have to realize that you are assuming a degree of risk that your traveling partners will interrupt your travel. One set of travelers I know had decided to travel together through Central and South America. A crash in Peru resulted in a broken collarbone. The crashed rider voted to cancel the rest of the trip and return to Colorado while his wingman wanted to settle down and wait for the bone to mend, or leave the bikes in Lima, fly home, then return after the bone had knitted. Rider A won out, in part because Rider B did not want to ride alone. Both packed up their gear and bikes and shipped them home. Five years later Rider B was still lamenting the fact his tour had been cut short, but had to have some solace in knowing he had been a good wingman and not left his buddy. The risk of having his tour cut short or canceled

This female American tourer managed North and South America, then Europe, and started into Africa before crashing hard enough to stop her attempt to ride around the world, solo. She was escorted home to Chicago, no longer able to travel on her own due to broken legs and malaria.

You are responsible to, and for, no one other than yourself.

had outweighed his personal need to have company versus going solo.

One factor often overlooked when choosing to tour with someone else is that you are accepting a certain amount of responsibility for those with you. A pair of riding pals decided to share their tour to Alaska. One crashed and broke a leg on the Dalton Highway headed to Deadhorse. His buddy got him into a hospital in Fairbanks then said, "I've got the rest of my vacation to enjoy. See you back in Colorado," and rode off into the midday sun. The rider with the broken leg was left to deal with not only flying back to Colorado but also shipping his bent and broken fully loaded touring bike. Had it not been for a "Good Samaritan" BMW dealer in Fairbanks, the downed rider would have had a monumental task. Needless to say, he and his riding buddy are no longer best buddies. Where one had assumed each would share some responsibilities, the other had shunned his in deference to his vacation being his priority.

WHEN TO STOP?

When two or more are touring together there is always the group consensus or vote to be taken as to when to stop for gas, food, and where to camp or motel for the night. This is often a time-consuming process and

SELFISHNESS

Some would argue selfishness when the preference to not share experiences is given as a reason for going solo, but the solo rider does not care. As one rider said to me when I asked why he was going around the world alone, "It's my money, my vacation, and my adventure. I chose not to share the experiences that I have worked so hard to enjoy. I doubt any riding partner I might have along would have worked, planned, or saved as hard as I did for this adventure, so we would be placing different values on what we get out of our investment." There is a certain amount of satisfaction in having worked for and successfully finished a ride that is savored more alone than having to share with someone else.

This motorcyclist was touring solo but hooked up with a group I was guiding for a few days. He rode at a slower pace than our group did. We would have to stop and gas-up while he would keep motoring, getting much better mileage at his slower speed. We would meet each night at our designated campground. When I asked if he would consider riding with another person or group, he said, "No way. It's my ride. I don't want to share it."

I met this rider touring Russia, solo, on a 500-cc motorcycle. Here I caught up with him again as he was touring America. He had shifted to a larger motorcycle to ride the super-slab highways and opined that he also had room for a passenger should he meet one, but said, "No dogs, thank you."

A final consideration in going alone is the sense of accomplishment you receive from having successfully completed your tour on your own, not having depended on others to aid or assist you.

PILLION

Definition: A passenger riding on the back of a motorcycle.

Who says "bigger is better"? This couple had been roaming around Central and South America when I met them in Chile. Their choice of motorcycle was a 500-cc Honda. She was the navigator and he was the pilot. He said, "When we're lost we know who is to blame, and it's not me."

often leaves one or more riders unhappy with the decision. The solo rider is free from these stops by the side of the road.

Another factor to consider when riding in a group is the fact that gas stops will be dictated by the rider with the smallest gas tank, as he will need fuel first. The rider with the 2 1/2-gallon gas tank can easily need twice as many pit stops in a day of riding as the rest of the group, thereby eating into the daylight riding time and number of miles attainable each day. This can be extremely frustrating to others in the group who are not ready to stop. For the solo rider, he can only be frustrated with himself for not choosing a motorcycle with a larger gas tank.

One advantage to solo touring is meeting more people. If you are stopped by the side of the road, local people will much more readily approach you and ask if you are lost or need help. If they see two or more people they assume you can figure out the problem. The same goes for being invited to stay in a person's home for the night; a solo rider will be asked more quickly than will a group of two or more. In a restaurant, if you are having dinner alone others will more quickly approach you. In a campground, those around you will be quicker to try and engage you in conversation than if you are alone.

A final consideration in going alone is the sense of accomplishment you receive from having successfully completed your tour on your own, not having depended on others to aid or assist you. Whether a weekend tour or a 'round-the-world ride, that sense of accomplishment does not have to be shared with another or a group. It is a validation that you are able to manage your ride independent of others.

TWO OR MORE

The "two-up" tour is when the pilot adds a pillion, or passenger, on the back of the motorcycle. This type of tour has several advantages and disadvantages.

Larger motorcycles allow more room for both the pilot and the passenger, as well as options like intercom systems, radio/CD players, and considerably more luggage-carrying capacity. On a big bike like this BMW LT, "comfort" is the focus of the ride, from suspension to wind protection to seating. This model also had an electric seat warmer!

First and foremost is the weight factor. Adding an additional 200 pounds to the back of the motorcycle can well exceed the load limits of the motorcycle. It may also drastically affect the handling of the bike.

Depending on the size and suspension of the motorcycle, the additional weight (especially that of the passenger who sits up high and counters the theory of keeping weight down low, thus lowering the center of gravity) can adversely affect stability and handling. A 1,000-pound touring bike, such as a Honda Gold Wing or Harley-Davidson Road King, may hardly notice the additional weight, whereas the 500-pound sport-touring model may have its handling radically affected in a negative manner.

A second consideration when carrying a pillion is your responsibility to their safety and security. The pillion is the responsibility of the pilot and should be recognized as a serious one. Your passenger's life is literally in your hands and if you cannot accept that responsibility, then you should leave the pillion at home.

Additionally, while you may be able to ride for hours without stopping, the pillion is often less able to do so. While the pilot may be protected from the wind by the motorcycle's fairing, the pillion might be suffering from wind buffeting. While on the back of the motorcycle, they have less opportunity for movement and shifting of weight than the pilot, thus adding to the need to stop and stretch more often. These stops can distract the pilot as well as cut into the riding day.

I once heard a naïve rider comment to his buddy's girlfriend after she complained about sore muscles, "What are you sore from? All you have to do is sit on the back." This rider had obviously never ridden far on the back of a motorcycle and had no appreciation for how taxing the work is for a good pillion.

GROUP RIDING

Asking your buddy or riding friends to join you on their motorcycles for a tour is a way to enjoy riding your motorcycle without the added weight of a pillion. But again, there are risks that must be weighed against the rewards.

I once agreed to go along with two friends on a ride to Alaska. I had ridden with each short periods of time, such as a Sunday ride, and thought them to be safe and reasonable riders. However, once we got on the road I soon learned we had some irreconcilable differences in riding styles, different enough that I decided to go it alone. One rider crashed on the second day while riding parallel to us on a deserted dirt road at high speed. Luckily,

Depending on the size and suspension of the motorcycle, the additional weight can adversely affect stability and handling.

GROUP RIDING

Asking your buddy or riding friends to join you on their motorcycles for a tour is a way to enjoy riding your motorcycle with other people without the added weight of a pillion.

A popular option for more spirited riders is a sport-touring bike like this Buell S3T. Such bikes provide a decent amount of comfort while maintaining a quick pace when the roads turn twisty. *Darwin Holmstrom*

While touring with others can reduce some risks, it can increase others.

"You are who you ride with."

RIDE

Choosing to ride with others on a tour is a commitment to the group and their goals. Before leaving on the tour, all parties should be in agreement with those goals to ensure some harmony in the ride.

the only serious damage done was when his head hit his windscreen and his glasses came apart. Damage to the motorcycle was mostly cosmetic and repaired with glue and duct tape.

In the days following his crash I noticed that he would often speed up and ride past me, while at other times he rode on either the left or right side behind me, often in my same track. At other times he would drop back so far I could no longer see him in my mirrors.

Seven days into our month-long trip he crashed again, this time while leading our group. Rather than slowing for railroad tracks in the rain, he angled across them. Had a car been coming in the opposite direction, I would have had to make a sad telephone call to his wife that night.

At lunch after the crash I suggested he should try riding at a more sedate speed and follow the other two of us in an assigned track. His response was, "Look, I've been riding motorcycles for over 20 years and I'm still alive, so I must be doing something right or I wouldn't be here. Greg, you don't know everything."

I had to agree with him on both counts and said that from that point on I would ride alone each day and meet him and his pal at the agreed upon campground at night. That was how we completed our trip. I had decided that I did not want to risk danger to myself by having him around me during the riding day while his partner was more willing to assume that risk.

On another occasion I agreed to ride to Sturgis with a female rider from Slovenia. Soon after we started she complained that I was riding too slow, suggesting that I was

afraid to ride faster. I calmly explained I was riding two to three miles per hour above the posted speed limits and that was close enough not to get a speeding ticket. She laughed and said she was not afraid of getting stopped. I then told her that while she might be able to talk herself out of a ticket with her smile, generous cleavage, and Slovene driver's license, I was certain to get ticketed with my American license. She called me a chicken, hoping to get me to abandon logic and common riding sense.

Several miles later I was slowing on a two-lane road as a car in front of me slowed and pulled slightly to the right. I could see the driver looking at a driveway into a farm on the left. My lady riding companion pulled out from behind me and whizzed past both the car and myself just as he started to make a left turn. She got by both of us and sped off down the road. To show me she could ride faster than I, she did not slow down and that was the last time that day I saw her. When she called my answering service some hours later and we made telephone contact, she laughed and asked if I was mad because I could not catch her. I did not give an answer.

That night at our campground I told her she could lead at any speed she wanted the next day because I did not want her behind me doing foolish things. And if she wanted to speed I would meet her at our next campground, which I did. That was how we finished our ride to Sturgis and then on into Denver, each going at our own pace and in our own style.

Choosing to ride with others on a tour is a commitment to the group and their goals.

Before leaving on the tour, all parties should be in agreement with those goals to ensure some harmony in the ride. If one person wants to stop and visit all of the castles on the route while another only wants to stop for food and gas, then either an agreement should be reached or the team should break up.

I once agreed to make a winter tour to Mexico with an American rider who had never ridden outside the United States. We both shared the desire to ride in the winter, when the Colorado snows had most riders housebound. We also both rode similar motorcycles and each had a good working knowledge of the mechanics of the bikes. Additionally, we each had road-raced motorcycles and shared an enthusiasm for the sport of motorcycle racing. The plan to make a three-week tour together seemed to be a good one.

Shortly after we arrived in Mexico it became apparent our travel styles were quite different. Whereas I was content to sleep and eat in lower budget places, my pal was used to the mid- to upper-level budget categories. When we stopped at the end of a day in front of a motel, I would ask him if it looked OK and he would say it was. At dinner and the next morning he would jokingly complain but would never accept the responsibility for having agreed to where we slept.

Finally, we arrived at a solution that seemed to work well for both of us. Each day one of us would be the decision-maker and leader, making all decisions on when to stop for gas, where to eat and sleep, and the pace of our riding day. Our trip soon became more fun as I could complain about his decisions and the next day he could complain about mine.

To his credit, he soldiered on at my lower budget style of touring. Upon the completion of our tour he did laughingly say that if he ever went to Mexico with me again he would carry a large box of supplies in a top-box that would have items for the rooms I picked. These would include a light bulb for the ones

Rather than two people on one bike, an option is for each person to ride their own. This American couple worked their way around the world on matching Harley-Davidsons. I met them in Germany, then later in Asia. He maintained the equipment and she managed their money, sleeping, and eating.

This German lady tourer had done most of the world solo. Not chasing any records or writing a book, she chose to tour by herself because she had the freedom to choose her own routes and times of the year she wanted to tour. She once crashed in the desert of Mexico and a group found her wandering in a daze with a concussion. She had forgotten her name for a spell. They dusted her off, re-attached her saddlebags, and she road off alone following the sun.

One bad apple had spoiled what had been a rather nice outing.

missing or not working in our room lamps, a toilet seat, and maybe even a toilet on which to put the seat. We have since traveled together outside the United States, and he has learned to adjust to a world without a Holiday Inn or Denny's all-you-can-eat breakfast.

While touring with others can reduce some risks, it can increase others. The idea that both you and your riding buddy each have the same kind of motorcycle lends some degree of security. If your motorcycle breaks down, your buddy may know how to make a roadside repair. On the other hand, if his motorcycle breaks down you are left with having to stick with him while repairs are made, which sometimes means days or weeks.

Another risk is joining with someone who is incompatible or unfriendly, bringing stress into your ride. It is not easy to tell someone you do not want to ride with them any farther; so most often you will stay together, no matter how uncomfortable the choice may be.

There was a book written by newbie traveler Andres Carlstein about his experience riding with two other experienced tourers through Mexico, Central, and South America called *Odyssey to Ushuaia*. After their tour was finished he expressed wonderment at why he had not been invited to one pal's wedding or heard anything from the other.

They had never met him before other than through the Internet, and when he first rolled into the parking lot of their motel before crossing the border into Mexico he was without his motorcycle title, an absolute necessity for travel outside the country. That error caused an immediate delay in their departure. His later antics on the road and at night soon had him often riding alone, and with little wonder. The book about his ride is probably one of the best examples of why not to go with someone else, and especially someone you have not toured with before. I would have left him at the Mexican border, whereas his two Internet pals chose to stick out their decision to tour as a group.

"You are who you ride with" is a quote from one of my earliest touring tutors. He told me this after we had an uncomfortable confrontation with a disgruntled camper who complained about the noise our bikes made. There were five of us in the group, four riding quiet motorcycles and one who had loud exhaust pipes. When the noisy one returned from town late in the evening he felt good enough to think the entire campground would like to hear his entry. He revved his engine numerous times as he coasted through camp, then several more times as he stopped and before he shut it off. In the morning all five of us were given a loud lecture about how rude bikers are, how

I found this group of Americans in Germany. They had traveled as a group across Asia and Europe. Here, their guide gives them instructions on how to put up their tents, good information if you are a novice camper/traveler. Their tour had been sleeping in pre-booked hotels up until this point.

inconsiderate and how ungentlemanly. The one bad apple had spoiled what had been a rather nice outing, and the lecture is still fresh in my mind.

Another example of this theory in practice happened while guiding a Guinness Record seeker across India. She crashed her motorcycle after applying too much front brake as two girls on a bicycle crossed in front of her, also causing the girls to crash. As I tried to lift up the downed BMW F650 lying in the middle of the road, the owner screamed at the two young girls. She picked up their bicycle, threw it off the road then hit and spit on the girl who was bleeding. It was a sad reflection on BMW riders and foreign motorcyclists as a whole. To the gathered open-mouthed crowd who watched this unfold I was as guilty of this unforgivable and foolish act as was the perpetrator because, while I was struggling with the downed motorcycle, I had done nothing to prevent the act from happening. It still bothers me today that I could not have done anything to prevent this incident and that I was associated with it. It was my choice to be with that riding partner so I must bear the weight of that decision, one that I have not made again.

One of my touring friends chose to make a ride with several other Americans into Mexico. Two of the others were typical of what would be called "ugly Americans." They were loud and boisterous and he complained that he did not like to be around them, and yet a year later had agreed to make a second ride with them. When I asked him why, if he knew that associating with them was a reflection on him, he said, "I'll ride alone during the day." When I asked about dinner, in their common motel and at lunch, he said, "Going with them is better than staying at home. I don't want to go alone. I like having someone I can talk to, so I'll just put up with them." *Yes*, I thought, *and the Mexican people will have to put up with a bigger crowd of noisy Gringos, you being one of them.*

GUIDED TOURS

A final touring option is to sign on with one of the increasingly popular guided tours.

These tours can range from a ride down Route 66 to a ride around the world. The tours put you together with others who simply want to ride motorcycles and leave the planning to the tour operator. Many sign on to these tours believing an organized group is safer than going it alone. This is a false sense of security, as most experienced touring riders will argue that as you increase the number in your group from one to more you also increase the risk of something going wrong. This is multiplied for riders you have never ridden with before or whose riding style is incompatible with yours. For instance, one rider on a 'round-the-world tour crashed in Russia and the two riders following behind him crashed into him.

An experienced tourer knows that being around or in a group of other riders he has never ridden with before is not a riding situation he wants to find himself in.

The result: one dead, one lost leg, and all three flown home. One of my tour operator friends says of his clients, "They have more money than brains." An experienced tourer knows that being around or in a group of other riders they have never ridden with before is not a riding situation they want to find themselves in. On one tour of Mexico the tour guide finally took the motorcycle away from a rider who crashed too often!

I once saw a man do something incredibly stupid, and as he was doing so I told him, "You know, what you are doing is a reflection of your personal decision-making capability." He kept on doing his stupidity. Later, someone asked me why I was of the opinion he was "the stupidest BMW rider in the world, and has proven to me by his actions that money neither purchases nor

It was my choice to be with that riding partner so I must bear the weight of that decision, one that I have not made again.

GRAND TOUR

Definition: An extended tour of continental Europe once considered a rite of passage for young wealthy English gentlemen.

The "fastest man around the world on a motorcycle" rides alone, unless he is leading one of his "around the world tours." Once around the globe on an Enfield, solo, twice around the world on a bicycle, solo, and then a 31-day solo record ride on a Triumph has taught him how to best manage his time and distances.

reflects intelligence or basic everyday common sense," I said, "Ask him." And the inquirer did, only to be told it "has nothing to do with my riding motorcycles." This response implied there's some pill or switch a poor decision maker can take to change their basic decision-making capability before starting their motorcycle. The last I heard he was a guide for an organized tour group.

A longtime tour operator once had a group of 40 for a guided tour. He knew the risk of riding in such a large group and broke it up into many smaller groups of three and set them off minutes apart each morning.

One of my acquaintances new to motorcycle touring has signed up for several guided tours and found them all to be satisfying. He readily admits being afraid to tour alone and unknowledgeable in planning and executing rides on his own. He also admits

For many touring motorcyclists, these tours are the only way they will ever tour away from home.

to knowing little about motorcycle maintenance and not wanting to learn. For him the satisfaction of touring comes from sitting in the bar of the upscale hotel at night and sharing tales and talk with fellow Americans on the tour, then recounting his adventures when he returns home. When he is asked if he knows he's spent five to ten times the cost of making the same tour on his own, he says the premium is what he pays for security, planning, comfort, and companionship. And this is a perfectly valid argument for choosing guided tours over solo trips.

I have worked as a tour guide, organized tours, participated in tours, and I've occasionally designed custom tours for select groups or individuals. For many touring motorcyclists, these tours are the only way they will ever tour away from home. For some it is a matter of time constraints and wanting to get the most riding possible. Others are afraid to go alone and need the security of a group. Others simply do not want to be bothered with the adventure (risk) of not having a comfortable bed, a chocolate on the pillow, guaranteed room reservations, American-style meals, and someone to carry their luggage.

Guided tours have been compared to what the Imperial Brits once called the Grand Tour. This was when the rich, young Brits journeyed to the Continent and visited the Right Places during the Right Time wearing the Right Clothes and wanted to be seen with the Right People. Today there is a certain amount of this Rightness coming from an ever-increasing circle who like to drop the fact that they have just returned from touring China, Africa, or New Zealand. It is a statement that you have money and can afford the time to expand your claims to have toured more, or wider than your neighbor Mr. Jones. Fortunately, there are guided motorcycle tours today to almost any place on the planet making the Right Ride possible. As the ad says, all you need is your credit card.

LONE WOLF OR BUDDYING UP?

While I generally try to avoid the herd mentality that accompanies touring with others, I have found some of my most memorable tours have been made with friends. Before my best friend got married, he and I would set aside a week or two each summer to make a long ride. Those rides were often the high point of our summers and I planned my work around them, as did he. We could bond, make jokes to each other, and share the camaraderie of motorcycle touring in a way I could not do alone.

While I have joined with others for short periods of time while riding around the world, I have often found this joining to be less than satisfactory. Usually whomever I joined up with had a far different riding style, budget, and personal program. One global traveler I traveled with had as her primary goal to secure as much publicity for herself as possible. Another lived by the *Lonely Planet Handbook*, wanting to see and do everything listed. Obviously, for me, with riding as much as possible being my goal, these joint tour periods were frustrating rides.

The primary decision comes down to responsibility and whether you want to be responsible only for yourself or take on the responsibility of being with others. Not to accept that responsibility is irresponsible in itself if touring with others, and I would not like to travel with someone so irresponsible. Irresponsible touring should not be done.

Man's best friend. This rider decided to tour with his best friend, his dog. I caught up with them as they were crossing South Dakota on their way to Sturgis.

Another man touring with his best friend. Known as "Lew and Punky," they toured from Florida to Alaska, then turned around and rode to the bottom of South America. Along the way they added a girlfriend who became a wife. Sadly, the day I took this picture in Moab, Utah, Punky ended up in the dog hospital, having been run over by a car.

EQUIPMENT, PILOT, AND PASSENGER READINESS:
KNOW YOUR LIMITS

WHAT YOU WILL LEARN

- How to select the best touring motorcycle for your needs and comfort

- What steps to take at home and on the road to prepare for unfortunate situations

- Financial, mechanical, physical, and mental readiness

One of my "luxo-rides" was this Harley-Davidson Ultra Classic. While it was ultra-comfortable moving across the super-slabs of America, like sitting in a recliner, it hated anything off-pavement. Whether a gravel road or a grassy footpath, the Harley wanted to try and lay down. It almost refused to be photographed in this sand shot.

What's the best touring motorcycle? Whatever you are comfortable with.

EQUIPMENT

"What is the best touring motorcycle?" That is one of the most commonly asked questions in motorcycle touring. If you ask a motorcycle salesman, he will have a whole line of answers ranging from "an adventure tourer" to "a sport tourer," depending on the make of motorcycle he sells. Ask a rider touring the world by motorcycle and they will probably tell you it is the brand and model they are riding. Ask a motorcycle journalist and he will probably have an answer 180 degrees from the next journalist.

My answer to that question is, "Whatever you are comfortable with," and not just sitting on. What's the best touring motorcycle? Whatever you are comfortable with.

Purchasing what a manufacturer markets as the "ultimate touring machine" does not ensure that it is the best. Advertising agencies are paid millions each year to get the message into your head and bring you closer to purchasing that machine. Often what the manufacturer and the advertising agency are saying has little correlation with your body, budget, and riding style. As an example, merely look at the large number of products sold as touring accessories such as taller windscreens, carrying bags, and after-market seats for touring motorcycles. Very few riders are satisfied with any motorcycle left in perfectly stock condition. Your comfort and personal taste will dictate how you modify your bike.

A clothing store has a wide variety of sizes of clothing to accommodate our various lengths and girths. Not so for motorcycles, although some do have adjustments for seat height, wind screen angle, and handlebar position. The designers and marketers are charged with producing a generic model mass-produced for as wide a market as possible. The clothing manufacturer knows they cannot produce generic one-size-fits-all clothing. Economically, however, this is

Three of my 'round the world touring motorcycles. The Kawasaki never burped once in a ride around the world. The BMW burped several times, leaving me stranded in some of the worst places on the globe, like Bogota, Colombia, when the front page of the newspaper was decrying American political involvement in that country. The 1947 Indian Chief toured America, burping almost daily. A 300-mile day on the Indian was equivalent to a 1,000-mile day on the Kawasaki in terms of achieving a daily mileage goal.

the only possible way to manufacture touring motorcycles.

One of my priorities for a touring machine is that it be something I am comfortable riding for long periods of time at speeds about 50 miles per hour, usually ranging from two to three hours at a time. For me this rules out anything where I have to hang on to the handlebars without the benefit of a windscreen keeping me from being blown off the back. In short, I prefer a plastic windscreen up front to deflect wind, rain, snow, bugs, birds, and sand over and around my upper body.

Several of the motorcycles I have purchased for touring came with factory-installed windscreens. Unfortunately, whichever gnome was designing the windscreens must have thought I was nearly the height of a chimpanzee because both windscreens were so low and small all they did was deflect wind onto my chest and pushed me toward the rear of the motorcycle at any speed above 35 miles per hour. At interstate speeds I had to lean over the gas tank to keep from having a perpetual smile blown on my face or my helmet ripped off.

The solution to my windscreen problems came in the form of aftermarket windscreens, with the factory-offered ones ending up in the spare parts bin of my work studio. I was able to select from varying heights and widths, as well as varying prices.

"Budget" comfort means how much I can comfortably afford. Faced with the option of going into serious debt versus riding debt

free, I prefer the comfort of touring debt free, and therefore try to fit my choice of motorcycle into my budget lifestyle.

I once toured America with a huge touring motorcycle, one of the most expensive on the market. While I loved the radio, plush seat, full fairing, and factory-offered carrying capacity, I reeled at the monthly payment schedule, insurance requirements, and cost of warranty maintenance. I also found the weight of nearly 1,000 pounds tiring when riding anywhere at slow speeds like trying to ride a greased pig off pavement.

My decision to move to a smaller, more lightweight motorcycle for my next long tour found me moving away from 1,200- to 1,800-cc engines and $20,000 to $25,000 price

I captured this world-famous traveler, writer Ted Simon, eyeing my touring motorcycle and scratching his head in wonderment. He had toured the world on a Triumph in the 1970s. After seeing my choice of touring machine, he struck out to tour the world again following his original path, this time on a BMW outfitted nearly the same as the one I caught him studying in this photograph.

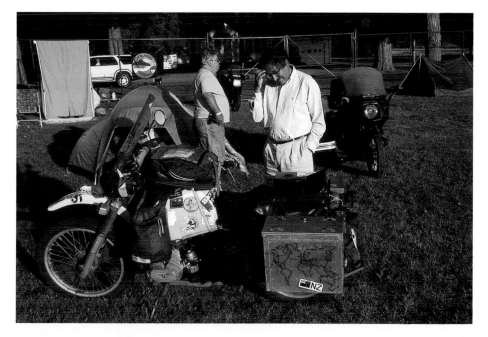

An Amazonas motorcycle from Brazil, with a factory sidecar. This Brazilian touring motorcycle was the largest motorcycle in the world when it was produced. Powered by a Volkswagen engine with a reverse gear, the owner said it could manage both highway and off-road touring. I used one of these rare motorcycles to do touring in South America and found it to be big and fun.

Make sure your insurance is paid up through the period of time you will be touring.

range into a budget category that would leave me enough money to make my tour.

With the larger, more expensive models, I also learned I was attracting more attention than I wanted, whether from unsavory locals wanting to relieve me of money, or authorities wanting to do the same because I looked like I had money.

My personal riding style also merited a choice far different from a 1,000-pound interstate behemoth. If I wanted to take routes that included a significant degree of gravel or mud, I would be more comfortable on a dual-purpose or dual-sport model, something that would handle gravel and mud more easily than the heavyweight tourer.

The possibility of losing my touring motorcycle also came into the decision-making process. Whether loss from theft, collision, or confiscation, I have learned that I do not want to take a motorcycle on a tour that I cannot afford to lose.

As I looked at the range of motorcycles offered in the 650-cc dual-sport range, I found a good number of choices. I could pay nearly $9,000 for a BMW 650-cc single, or $5,000 for a Japanese model. In the end, I opted for the $5,000 choice, using the difference between that and the BMW for accessories and two and a half months of life on the road, a budget consideration with which I could live. I would have spent the same amount on accessories for either motorcycle

BMWs are a favored touring machine known for their reliability. This red bike looked to be a nice mix between an interstate cruiser and a canyon carver. The one thing I have learned about red motorcycles is they stand-out, making them quite photogenic but also radar-genic to the police.

This European rider chose a sportbike to tour the world. There was no room on the back for a passenger. The short handlebars made off-road riding very difficult, but he had managed the mud-wallows through the Congo and the sands of the Sahara.

to make each comfortable, but forgoing image for a better life on the road met my budget comfort consideration.

PILOT AND PASSENGER READINESS

Trying to anticipate what to expect while touring is an art. One beginner went so far as to make plans in case he was captured and held for ransom. Doubtless this is beyond the scope of any normal preparedness most of us will ever need. In his case, his foolishness was rewarded when his plans were needed after he was taken hostage. While it is not known what his self-insurance costs were, what is known is that he planned for its need.

INSURANCE READINESS

Insurance is a good start for readying yourself for your tour. Make sure your insurance is paid up through the period of time you will be touring. This applies to both your personal health insurance and your vehicle insurance.

If touring outside the United States, determine whether you will have vehicle coverage. For instance, if your tour is through Canada to Alaska, check with your insurance carrier to see if you will have coverage outside the country and whether your liability insurance is good in Canada. If not, you may find you have to purchase

Canadian third-party insurance at the border before entering Canada.

The same holds true of other countries, such as Mexico. You will find that liability insurance is required for riding in Mexico and that your American insurance policy is not in effect once you cross the border. Therefore, you will have to purchase Mexican insurance at the border to legally ride in Mexico.

I was once told by a Mexican insurance agent, after purchasing an expensive liability insurance policy from him, that if I

In the early days of motorcycle touring, a rider simply added a Vetter Windjammer fairing and a king-queen saddle to create an instant touring bike. Extended forks were optional. *Darwin Holmstrom*

A fully prepped touring motorcycle and smiling rider at the beginning of a long-distance touring rally. Several days later the rider crashed out of the event. While some would argue that "preparation is everything" in long-distance touring, there is little riders can do to prepare for a crash. Most try to ignore thinking about the possibility.

Just how good is your medical insurance and where are the limits?

was involved in an accident, no matter whose fault it was, I would be best off settling with the other driver and getting away as quickly as possible. He explained that Mexican law (and much of the world's law outside the United States) is based on Napoleonic Law, which says you are guilty until you prove yourself innocent. Therefore, if involved in an accident, you, the foreigner, are guilty until you prove yourself innocent. While trying to do so with the help of a Mexican lawyer, you may find the process lengthy and expensive, and your vehicle may be impounded until the process is complete. Sometimes it is not worth the expensive effort to prove yourself innocent and you are better off abandoning the impounded motorcycle. The usual argument put forth by the locals in these cases is that the accident was your fault because it would not have happened had you, the foreigner, not been in their country.

Many riders are surprised to find they cannot purchase theft coverage for their motorcycle in the country they are planning to tour. Another surprise is how expensive it can be when it is available, often as much as 300 to 400 percent more than it costs in the United States.

Another factor to take into consideration is the high cost of vehicle insurance as you move from one country to the next, even if only for a few days. When I entered Morocco I found that the European "Green Card" insurance I had purchased for Europe was not valid in Morocco. I had to purchase one-month's worth of Moroccan insurance for a price equivalent to what I had paid for two months of insurance for most of Europe.

As I moved around Europe and toward Russia I found other countries, such as Latvia, did not honor the German Green Card insurance I had purchased, and I was

required to pay for liability insurance at each border. One rider likened this country-by-country insurance as a road tax, the price I had to pay for using the roads of that country.

Also important is determining how much risk you are willing to assume. Rather than take the time to seek an insurance seller in countries where insurance is required but not demanded, like in Mexico, are you willing to assume the risk of touring without it, and the possible impounding of your motorcycle if you are caught without it?

I met a European couple riding across Russia. The pilot came from a country where he had little opportunity to ride on anything other than fine paved roads, so he had little experience on gravel. He also was concerned about how difficult the road heading east from Moscow was, telling me it was "2,000 kilometers of the Road to Hell." I ventured off alone, without insurance. He loaded his bike and pillion on a train in Moscow and limited the risks he was unprepared to assume.

Medical insurance is also an area of consideration for rider and passenger preparedness. More directly, just how good is your medical insurance and where are the limits? Are you prepared to assume the possible expense of medical coverage for you or your pillion if your insurance is not valid where you are touring?

One Swiss couple was touring California on a borrowed motorcycle when it had a flat tire. They crashed, causing severe injuries to the pillion on the back. The American owner of the motorcycle arranged a lawyer for the couple in representing their claims against his insurance company, which were eventually settled for a large sum, the lawyer receiving one third and the couple receiving the remaining two-thirds. Luckily, the couple kept all but $1,000 of their portion, a nice supplement to the Swiss medical coverage all Swiss citizens have wherever they travel on the globe. This is not so for American citizens; in fact, we have no accident insurance anywhere unless we purchase it or it is purchased for us.

An older Japanese motorcycle still makes a fine touring mount, provided it's well-maintained and the owner doesn't mind sacrificing a certain amount of comfort and convenience.
Darwin Holmstrom

The one part of me I have never found easy to prepare for a long ride is my bottom. Many stock touring motorcycles come with uncomfortable seats. A custom seat, like on this BMW, has often proved to be one of the wisest investments a rider can make in preparing for a long ride. While expensive, many riders insist the price is worth it.

breaking his pelvis. At the Argentine hospital the staff contacted his private insurer (an HMO) in Denver, Colorado, to see if they would pay for his needed medical procedure. Instead, the HMO sent a private air medical ambulance to Argentina to collect the broken rider and return him to their facility in Denver. When his bills were totaled it came to more than $57,000, including the flight home. His portion was under $200. Unfortunately, the motorcycle tour operator had made no provision to carry a broken motorcycle so the client had to return a year later to collect his crumpled bike and ship it back to the United States.

MECHANICAL READINESS

If touring the United States, you can prepare for the broken bike problem with several roadside assistance plans like those offered through the American Motorcyclists Association, Harley Owners Group, or Motorcycle Towing Service. These plans will collect your motorcycle from the side of the road and can carry them considerable distances to your home or local dealer. I feel that if the rider is not well-trained enough to do basic roadside repairs, like fixing a flat, or if the motorcycle is too complicated or big, then these plans are as necessary as a valid driver's license.

If you have medical coverage but need to return to the United States to be treated, you may want to consider medical evacuation insurance. This is reasonably inexpensive and good for either you or your mortal remains to be returned by standard passenger airplane or medical ambulance back to your home-care provider. Some policies are also good within the United States and include shipping your motorcycle back to your home or local dealer.

One of my motorcycle acquaintances crashed while on a guided tour in Argentina,

An inexpensive alternative to the expense of a custom seat is a seat pad of sheepskin or beads as pictured. Some riders purchase a seat pad or beaded seat designed for an automobile and hand-cut it to fit their motorcycle. The difference between a custom seat and a personal modification can easily be between $400 and $500.

How well you and your motorcycle fit together is another area of preparedness. This means how the handlebars and levers are positioned, how your bottom fits to the seat, and the way your legs fold or stretch out. What feels or looks good in the garage can be hell on the road. A short two- or three-day test ride before you go will usually point out problems you can correct easily before you go.

Dealing with finances while touring is another preparedness factor.

Another thing I check on my test ride is how well my packing system works and how well the motorcycle handles with the touring weight. If the front end wobbles when I take my hands off the handlebars, I move weight forward and lower. If the motorcycle is unmanageable on gravel or off

pavement, I plan my route to avoid these sections. It is better to go 200 to 400 miles around a bad section than to break a leg (or worse) trying to physically manage an unmanageable motorcycle.

While you're out on the test ride, measure the mileage you are getting per gallon of gas as well as how many gallons of usable gas you have in your gas tank. One motorcycle I own advertises nearly 5 1/2 gallons of gas in the tank, but the last 1/2 gallon is unusable unless you lay the motorcycle on its side to slosh it into the left side of the tank. That means I have to deduct about 20 miles in my riding range versus what the manufacturer suggests the motorcycle can do, unless I want to stop, unpack, and lay the motorcycle over.

Having someone near your home base that can send you spare parts if needed is also a part of preparing, especially if leaving the country, where parts might not exist. They should be experienced enough with your motorcycle to know what you may need and how to get them to you. A little time together before you go discussing the

Before motorcycle manufacturers started offering factory-built touring rigs, aftermarket manufacturers offered stylish and effective fairings and saddlebags. *Darwin Holmstrom*

AFTERMARKET EQUIPMENT

Definition: Accessories sold by companies other than the original manufacturer of the motorcycle.

Honda was the first Japanese manufacturer to offer a purpose-built touring bike with standard touring accessories, the Gold Wing Interstate. That model was followed by the upscale Gold Wing Aspencade shown here. *Darwin Holmstrom*

options between Federal Express versus the U.S. Postal Service may save you days and many dollars if you need the help.

FINANCIAL READINESS

Dealing with finances while touring is another preparedness factor. One unhappy traveler found that his sole credit card was no good when he got to Mexico. His credit card company was unaware he was leaving the country and refused to honor charges they thought were possibly unauthorized. As he had little or no cash when he made the discovery, it was a long day of telephone calls to free up his card. I always call my credit card company before I leave on a tour and advise them where I am going and how long I will be gone.

I also keep a written record of the numbers and name on my card, and the number to call if the card is lost or stolen. Usually there is a toll-free number to call inside the United States and a regular number to call collect outside the country, since toll-free numbers do not work from foreign countries.

When my credit card went missing in Cali, Colombia, on Christmas Day it was nearly impossible to find an Internet café to contact the credit card company electronically and advise them of the loss. But after finding a telephone, it was reassuring to call the card company representative on the

Personal limitations are unique to each of us and vary with condition and age.

telephone and speak to a live person. The first question they asked was, "What is the number on your lost credit card?" I was able to kill the card within an hour of it going missing, and a replacement was in the mail the very next day. There are still times when a telephone number and a phone call beats the Internet.

I traveled once with a friend who had all his credit card information inside a computer. I asked what would happen if the computer died or was stolen. He looked at me aghast, like such a thing could not happen. It often does, so keep a well-hidden paper backup of your needed financial information and, of course, never keep your personal identification numbers with copies of your credit card or bank information.

I also have gone to another backup system on my credit cards: not being dependent on one credit card while traveling. Twice I have had my credit card eaten by ATM machines, once on a Friday night in Antigua, Guatemala. I had to wait until the bank opened on Monday before I could get the card back. The second time I was not able to get my card returned until I had completed a lengthy police report and my credit card company had faxed their approval back to the ATM owner, not something quickly done outside normal working hours.

Once I had a credit card "die" when my friend placed his magnetic tank bag on the bed in our motel room. He placed it on top of my coat, which held my wallet. The magnets in the tank bag deleted the information on my card's magnetic strip. Fortunately, my backup card was tucked away with other documents (like my original motorcycle title) in a safer place.

Do you have a back-up plan for when things go wrong? Before leaving on your tour, try to imagine everything that might go awry while you are away, then make and execute a back-up plan. For instance, who can you rely on to go to your house and break-up the party your kids are having for half the college campus while you are 1,000 miles away and called home to check on things? Or who has access to your medical records, insurance policy, will, or safe deposit box?

One of the things to prepare for is how to prevent loss or theft. Innumerable hours or days can be spent trying to replace a lost wallet or passport. I carry two wallets, one is

FANNY PACK

A lazy man's way of saying to the world, "Here is where you can find my valuables."

Knowing your motorcycle's limits is part of the preparation for touring. I knew my motorcycle could make the 240 miles to Deadhorse, but only if I drove slowly to maximize my miles per gallon. Rather than take the slow way, I invested $5 in a plastic gas can to carry two extra gallons. That was far less expensive than paying $400, or as much as $1,000, for an aftermarket gas tank, and I only needed the extra gas on this one section of road. Usually I can find gas within a 200-mile stretch.

Sometimes you have to adjust your plans to accommodate riding conditions. If heading into a snowstorm or bad rain, think about putting the motorcycle in a truck or on a trailer. When coming to a stream too deep to cross, load the motorcycle on one elephant and yourself on the other. Smaller motorcycles are best suited for this kind of travel, but this elephant can carry an 800-pound bike. The trick is getting it onto the chair.

a "throw down" or what I will give to someone with a gun or knife who wants it. In it I have a few dead credit cards, fake driver's license, business cards from others, and a few dollars of local currency. In my other wallet I have what is absolutely necessary, like my valid driver's license, one credit card, and enough cash for the day. The rest of my valuables I keep stashed in my clothing, on the motorcycle, or in some other hard-to-find place.

I never carry valuables in a fanny pack. While a fanny pack is convenient, I view it as a lazy man's way of saying to the world, "Here is where you can find my valuables." The same holds true for a backpack. In it I carry nothing valuable, only what I can afford to lose. In France I saw four young

men surround a tourist on a street corner and in a matter of seconds push him down and cut off his fanny pack and run before I could get across the street to help him. Gone in five seconds—that's how easy and how long it took.

Whether going away for two days or six months, try to project what might come up while you are away and take care of it before you leave

I once met a traveler in India who had set his backpack down just long enough to put on a jacket. When he reached back down the backpack was gone, along with all his valuables, including his wallet, passport, and travelers checks. We met at the American embassy where he was nearly crying because they could replace his passport, but only if he paid for passport photos and a processing fee. His having no money and their not giving or lending him any was the source of his frustration. I lent him $100 so he could get a room, a meal, and make a few telephones calls back to the United Stares, plus get his new passport. While I may never see the $100, I did have the satisfaction of knowing he would never carry valuables in a backpack again.

If I am going to walk around town for some time, I put my passport or wallet on the inside of my jeans where I have sewn some inside pockets. I do not carry anything valuable in my outside pockets other than some walking around cash. To get my valuables someone is going to have to cut my pants off, which was once tried when I crashed in Brazil! That time I regained consciousness before the truckers were able to get the job done.

CELL PHONES

While I do not carry a cell phone when traveling inside the United States (or anywhere else), I do carry a telephone credit card.

Some places I tour inside the United States still do not have cell connections, but I am still able to find pay phones just about everywhere. In an emergency, when I cannot find a pay phone I can usually find someone who is carrying a cell phone that will make a call for me if I pay for the call. For some riders the security of having a cell phone for emergencies offsets the expense and additional wires and weights. Normally, I add a cell phone to the "gizmo" list, something I have lived without for over a million miles but could move to the "needed list" if I had the space and money.

I once toured with a cell phone junkie who had to make calls and take calls whenever we stopped. In the evening he would spend at least an hour on his cell and it would ring until he turned it off to go to

Mental preparation should also include adjusting your mental thinking to being away from the security of your home base.

sleep. It was like he had taken his office, friends, and girlfriend with him on the tour. He was frantic when we got to Coldfoot, Alaska, where he discovered there was no cell service. I asked him why he had even bothered with the time and expense of making our tour if all he could think about was his calls. His response was, "I needed the time away." I thought, "Away from what?" I know I was glad to get away from him and his telephone as I often found myself wasting riding time waiting for him to finish his phone calls. He had not prepared himself for quality touring and time away if he had not found a way to become detached from his electronic umbilical cord.

PHYSICAL AND MENTAL READINESS

The physical side of being prepared for a tour can take several forms. I usually try to

get in a long weekend on my touring bike before I depart, breaking in my back, neck, arms, and buttocks. I try to make each of these test riding days at least 300 miles with a mix of riding from interstate to gravel. Not only am I easing my body back into the roll of long days on the motorcycle, but I am also looking for those things on the motorcycle that can be a nuisance once I am on the road. For instance, before leaving on my last long ride I acquired a new helmet. While it fit fine around the house, I found that it had an annoying habit of catching on the collar of my riding jacket when I turned

Know how to slow down when a car or truck approaches you from the opposite direction on a muddy road, then duck down below the windscreen as it passes. Loud pipes won't save your life in a situation like this, but wearing a helmet might, especially one with a face shield that you can flip up after the truck has gone by.

With their powerful six-cylinder engines capable of hauling just about any load, the Gold Wing continues to define the upper end of touring motorcycles. *Darwin Holmstrom*

my head to the right. Back at my studio after my test ride I took a file to the helmet's chin mechanism and rounded off a squared corner. This solved the problem.

Mental preparedness is another element of making a successful tour. In my knowledgeless youth I was mentally prepared for the foolishness of 1,000-mile days of riding, and once pushing that foolishness to 1,300 miles. With age comes wisdom, and now when I prepare my tour schedule I map out 300- to 500-mile days depending on riding conditions. I have also fine-tuned what I call my stupidity factor. Meaning I no longer feel I have to push on stupidly knowing I have nothing to prove by riding beyond reason and my physical limits.

Mental preparation should also include adjusting your mental thinking to being away from the security of your home base. On one tour of Mexico I was with another rider who could only complain about the Mexican culture. He complained about

their menus (being in Spanish), showers (only having marginal hot water at certain hours of the day), food (no hash browns with his breakfast), and mattresses (lumpy).

Preparing mentally means you should adjust your thinking.

His general comment was, "Why can't these people learn how to do things right, like we do back home?" I finally told him if he wanted things to be like they were back home he should keep his motorcycle touring confined to back home. He was not mentally prepared and adjusted to touring away from his lifestyle and the security of the American lifestyle.

Preparing mentally means you should adjust your thinking from what you are accustomed to toward experiencing what is different. Grits replace hash browns in the southern United States, and "Yawl" replaces "You all." In Peru, an American breakfast at a hotel means roll, jelly, juice, and coffee, not an all-you-can-eat breakfast buffet or the Denny's Breakfast Special. The adjustment will reduce your complaining, which is generally what unhappy people do, make your tour more enjoyable, and your presence more so to those around you. It also will often make you more appreciative of what you have back home when you get there.

Before leaving on your tour, make a photocopy of all your documents, including passport, driver's license, motorcycle registration, proof of insurance, and medical cards.

OTHER TIPS

Making sure that things "back home" are in order before you leave makes for a smoother tour. Whether going away for two days or six months, try to project what might come up while you are away and take care of it before you leave so you will not be dealing with it while on the road. This means bills coming due (like your monthly insurance premium), canceling the morning paper delivery, finding someone to water your plants, and giving them a spare set of house keys in case you cannot return as scheduled.

Before leaving on your tour, make a photocopy of all your documents, including passport, driver's license, motorcycle registration, proof of insurance, and medical cards. It is much easier to explain to a police officer that you do have a valid driver's license when yours is lost or stolen if you have a copy of your original to show him. With a copy of your lost passport and a couple of passport-size photos, it is usually pretty easy to replace a lost or stolen passport; but be prepared to answer a lot of questions. United States embassy and

"Sugar sand" in Africa. I was touring through Botswana when I came upon this section of road. It was slow going, and in the 110-degree temperature I soon realized I was dehydrated and nearly passing out. I carried 2 liters of water with me at all times in Africa and had to remind myself to drink water regularly throughout the day. The dry heat kept me from feeling sweat and thus knowing I was losing body fluid as I flogged my way through the sand.

KNOW YOUR LIMITS

Some riders seem to thrive on bagging 1,000-mile days when touring, most notably American riders. Some do it with considerable aid and assistance while others enjoy the effort as a solo attempt. The only times I have ever done those kind of miles was when I needed to be back to wife, school, office, or work, and although I was in good physical shape I found each experience painful. I once asked several of these long distance tourers what they found rewarding for all their preparation. The answers ranged from "joining the club" to "proving I can do it." When I asked them if they would do it if nobody knew they did it the answer was a universal "no."

Personal limitations are unique to each of us and vary with condition and age. I have found that starting out gently on a tour and working up to longer days lets my body toughen up as time goes on. Rather than try to bag a 600-mile day on Day 1, I go for 300 to 500 miles. This way I don't feel so beat-up at the end of the day that I have to sleep longer the next morning to make up for it. Toward the end of my tour I find I can more easily notch the longer days if I want, not paying the price of soreness and pain for the experience.

Taking personal measure of yourself during the riding day is an often overlooked necessity. I usually try to make lunch a snack rather than a large meal because afterwards, back on the road, the stomach doing its work on the heavy food can make me sleepy and less focused and therefore put me in a highly dangerous situation. If I do get tired or start to feel sleepy, I stop riding and take a short rest, or sometimes a nap, for a few minutes. One of my long distance riding friends calls these "power naps." I call them my meditation periods, although one lady friend traveling with me saw through that and said, "Heck, you're just old and tired, taking a nap." A short rest or nap can save you from making a small mistake at 70 miles per hour that can turn into a big error. I would rather be old and tired than young and dead.

I avoid caffeine while touring, especially during the middle of the day or when I feel sleepy. While caffeine in soda, coffee, or tea can give a temporary energy boost, it can also let you down very fast when it wears off. You often feel more tired afterwards than before. Another downside to caffeine is it is a diuretic, which means I will soon need to make a second restroom stop. Neither solves my problem of being sleepy or tired for long, so rather than create a problem with a solution, I just take the time to meditate and rest.

If you are not good at off-road riding you should be willing to throw in the towel and turn around when you reach the end of the pavement like I did here in Africa. A day or two in the Sahara with no water or food can easily result in death.

Knowing my limits has included the realization that I am not as fresh and strong in the afternoon as I am at the start of the day. A route decision I might make in the morning is often discarded in the afternoon. It took me some years to realize I have some physical weaknesses that manifest themselves more in the afternoon than in the morning, like tired knees and sore wrists. I know now to defer hard or risky sections of riding until I can best manage them safely. I also know that I have nothing to prove to anyone other than myself when touring and that there was truth in the fable of the tortoise and the hare.

Option 1 was to ride around this flooded road. Option 2 was to attempt to ride across. Option 3 was to wait until the floodwater subsided (a few hours to a few days). Had I made a mistake while riding across it I could well have been bobbing down this river into the Indian Ocean.

A short rest or nap can save you from making a small mistake at 70 miles per hour that can turn into a big error.

consulate employees are extremely inquisitive about lost or stolen American passports, more so now than ever before due to heightened terrorist activities worldwide.

When I leave the United States I file a power of attorney with my personal attorney naming him as the one who can sign for me while I am away. While I file that with him, I also make sure my will is current and that he has the latest copy. I do not plan on my demise on a tour, but I am a realist and know the possibility exists. The idea of some local judge deciding on the disposi-

tion of my assets with a third going to the state is enough of a nightmare to bring me back from the dead. I sleep better and tour more comfortably knowing my personal affairs are in order and my assets will go to whomever I choose. Too often I have watched others struggle with the estates of those who did not have their affairs in order, often robbing wives and children of what they needed to comfortably survive, when a rider did not prepare for the unthinkable.

While the touring pilot should go through the above in preparing to leave on a tour, the pillion should do the same. Any relationship can be strained to its limits when one in a party of two (or more) is not prepared. Imagine spending two or three weeks waiting for a replacement credit card to be sent, or dealing with local medical workers because one of the traveling team was not prepared.

Following Honda's success, other Japanese manufacturers started offering purpose-built touring motorcycles.

MAINTENANCE AND REPAIRS ON THE ROAD

WHAT YOU WILL LEARN

- **Planning ahead for routine repairs on the road**

- **Preparing a toolkit for repairs on the go**

- **Creative "out of the box" repairs for remote locations**

It can be a long, lonely day when your bike breaks down in the jungle and you can't make repairs by yourself. You can easily spend $1,500 to get your motorcycle towed back to a motorcycle shop or more to have it flown back to civilization. One broken driveshaft in Moab, Utah, cost a BMW owner nearly $1,500 for a rental truck to the nearest motorcycle shop, repairs, and time lost.

Being prepared like a good Boy Scout is one of the mottos not to be forgotten when touring. Whether it's purchasing a roadside assistance plan before leaving or being able to make the repairs yourself by carrying the right tools and spare parts, both can ease the pain of a breakdown on the road.

Experience has shown that certain models of BMW GS motorcycles experience Paralever driveshaft failure. The rule of thumb for these models is that once past the 30,000-mile mark you are riding on borrowed time. It was no surprise then to learn of a British rider who knowingly set off from Quito, Ecuador, with 30,000 miles on his speedometer who had his driveshaft fail in a small town in Peru where no parts were available. Thousands of BMW GS owners, including himself, could have said, "We told you so." All the stranded rider could do was find an Internet café, begin sending messages for help, and settle down for a long wait and the high expense of ship-

ping the replacement part. He had not done the routine maintenance of replacing the driveshaft that even he knew was eventually going to be needed.

There are some repairs that are nearly impossible to make while touring.

While not part of the motorcycle, I always add my rain suit, gloves, and helmet to my check list and make sure these parts of my touring kit are complete and in good working condition. The face-shield on my helmet can be easily replaced in Denver, Colorado, but not so easily in Bolivia, South America. The rain suit that leaked when I put it away after last using it has not since healed itself.

While I try never to start a tour with marginal tires, I know of several touring

To say that you should have your motorcycle in A-1 condition before departing is a given, but what that means varies from one rider to the next. Before leaving on a tour this is a minimal checklist of how I prepare my motorcycle:

- New fluids throughout
- New or near-new tires and tubes, pressure checked
- Fresh battery
- New brake pads, especially in the front
- Fresh bulbs, headlight/taillight
- New air cleaner
- Lube all cables
- Nut/bolt inspection to make sure everything is tight
- Complete tune-up

I also check my toolkit and spare parts to make sure I have not borrowed something out since the last ride and not returned or replaced it.

A DUCT TAPE FIX IS A SHORT TERM FIX

When making emergency repairs with duct tape, do not fool yourself into thinking it is anything more than a short-term fix. Wind, rain, heat, and time will cause the tape to deteriorate. Replace the duct tape fix with a permanent repair as soon as you can.

buddies who are content to ride their tires until bald and begin searching for a replacement wherever they are. They figure the time they lose hunting and replacing tires on the road is worth the money saved getting the most miles out of their tires. What they seldom figure in their equation is the fact that they could purchase the tires locally or through mail order for 20 to 50 percent less than what they pay on the road. They also fail to consider the safety factor, which is reduced as the tire wear increases.

As for regular maintenance items like light bulbs, fuses, and electrical tape, I do not expect the rest of the world to offer the same supplies as an American gas station. For instance, when touring through parts of the Yukon or many places in Mexico, about all one can reasonably expect to find in a gas station is gas, or possibly oil. If my motorcycle requires special oil, I carry it with me. The same goes for headlight bulbs.

There are some repairs that are nearly impossible to make while touring. For

A "gas station" in Laos. He could sell me gas and oil, but I was out of luck trying to get anything repaired. I carried a few spare electrical parts, a full set of tools, and a bag of mixed nuts and bolts. A broken spoke was welded, a set of vice grips fixed a broken clutch cable, and a punctured tube was patched.

A rural gas station in the Golden Triangle of Thailand. In much of the world, gas stations sell little more than gas and oil. Repairs on motorcycles are often made at motorcycle shops unfamiliar with expensive or "modern" motorcycles.

Basic knowledge of simple motorcycle mechanics should be required for anyone touring.

While electronic equipment can prove useful, one universal truth about motorcycle touring is that the more electronic equipment you have, the greater your odds of a malfunction. If one component in this high-tech dash failed, it could disable the entire motorcycle. *Darwin Holmstrom*

instance, if the transmission fails on your motorcycle it is doubtful that seals, gaskets, and gears will be easily found anywhere except your model's local dealership. In a Third World country, away from the security of your local shop, you may not even have the luxury of finding a motorcycle repair shop to make repairs on your bike.

I am constantly surprised when I meet the credit card tourers rolling around the globe who know little more than how to stick the key in their ignition or solve a roadside breakdown with a credit card. These are usually well-heeled riders who seem to care little for the loss of time and money when their motorcycle breaks or needs simple maintenance.

Knowing the simple mechanics of your motorcycle, like how to adjust your chain or

how gas gets from your gas tank to your engine, should be required for anyone touring. While motorcycle repair shops and dealerships are in the business to do maintenance service and repairs for you, the time lost to touring would seem to suggest the unprepared tourer is more interested in visiting these repair shops than touring.

I would add to the list of required skills the ability to check and change your own engine and drivetrain oil, how to repair a punctured tire, how to check and add engine coolant, and battery maintenance. All of these repair and maintenance items can be easily purchased at an auto parts store, if you can find one, and save you considerable time in trying to "credit card" a solution, especially in parts of the world that do not accept credit cards.

While I am a certified mechanic of some older models, I am probably better described as a reasonable shade tree mechanic on most. I do not purport to have much knowledge on newer computerized systems, and I limit my claims to knowing how electricity is made and turns into a spark plug spark or volts, amps, and watts. I carry a full repair manual with me on all my touring motorcycles, versus the one that came with the motorcycle when I purchased it. What I *can* claim is that I know how to read the manual and its electrical wiring chart and do so regularly. With these "know-how" tools in my personal tool bag I am often able to diagnose and repair many of the ills my motorcycles suffer from as I tour. However, when the model is one of the newer

An auto parts store in Russia. I actually found something here I needed: a hose clamp. At the end of each day the storeowner would pile his goods back into his truck and drive home.

In India there were many motorcycle repair shops, but nearly all were brand-specific to motorcycles sold in India. If the computer on a motorcycle had to be remapped, a mechanic with his laptop would have to be flown in from somewhere else, or the bike would have to be shipped to a shop able to solve the problem, most likely outside of India.

ones with computers, fuel injection, and optic cable wiring harnesses, I throw in the towel and vector into a local motorcycle dealer hoping they will have the part, a computer diagnostic system, and the knowledge needed to fix my ailing motorcycle.

On a recent tour around the United States, I discovered that most dealers have moved toward a minimal inventory management system. Rather than tie up needed capital by purchasing parts that often sit on the shelf for months or years at a time, they downsize their inventory to carry only what they need on hand and reduce carrying costs. They depend on overnight delivery services from central warehouses to supply them with replacement parts and accessories, including items one might expect them to carry at all times, like tires. This is more pronounced at the end of the riding season when their inventory might sit on the shelf through the winter until the spring.

During one of my rides to Alaska I learned from a local motorcycle dealer in Canada that they stocked up on tires in the spring and sold their stock down until the fall. They suggested that if I knew I would need a tire when I arrived I should order it through them about two weeks in advance so they would be sure to have it in stock when I arrived.

I recommend novice motorcyclists take a motorcycle maintenance course before starting off on a tour. These are relatively inexpensive, take only a few hours, and give the motorcyclist a minimal understanding

A mechanic once told me 90 percent of all motorcycle problems are electrical. I carry a wiring schematic, circuit tester, and spare electrical components. However, when a computer governs the electrical system I am at the mercy of the manufacturer and their dealer network. It is just too expensive to carry a replacement, and I have no idea how to make repairs to them. My option in those cases is to have available a good motorcycle towing service.

America's oldest Kawasaki dealership is found in Lander, Wyoming. I stopped to see how well it was stocked for parts. I was told, "What we don't have here we can have tomorrow sent in by overnight shipping. This is a nice town and food and sleeping is quite reasonable, not a bad place to spend some time." I had to agree with the mechanic.

REPAIR OR FIX A SLOWLY LEAKING TIRE IMMEDIATELY

A slowly leaking tire will not get well by repeatedly adding more air, and seldom does goop or snot added from a can solve the problem. When you have a slowly leaking tire it is a screaming wake-up call to make a permanent replacement ASAP. The accident you avoid will be your own.

Three options for breaking the bead on a tire by the side of the road: Top, a plastic wedge called a Bead Popper; bottom right, a 5-pound motorcycle tire clamp; bottom left, a woodworking C clamp. All three will do the job. I once had to cut an old tire off with a chisel and hammer. I now carry one of the three.

of how motorcycles work and how to do routine maintenance, like change a tire or plug a hole. If time does not permit a course, then I recommend the beginner spend some time with their maintenance manual and a motorcycle repair book before hitting the road. The simplest thing, like knowing how to replace a light bulb or adjust a chain can save not only time and money, but also the rider from having an accident if either go bad when needed.

One of the maintenance areas I spend more time on than others is on tires. Maybe that's because I have had flat tires and blowouts in some of the worst places in the world. Another reason is my background in road racing and my worrying about tire failure on the track.

When touring, I check my tires daily. That does not mean I walk by and glance at the tread depth. I get down on my tired and aching knees each morning, rotate the wheels and look at the whole tire, then check the tire pressure with my tire pres-

sure gauge. I have pulled out nails, screws, thorns, and wire from my tires countless times during these inspections, and a number of times I have found the tire pressure dangerously low. Taking off without having made those simple repairs could have found me spending my day unhappily working on the side of the road in rain, snow, or hot sun. With luck I may have been able to call a roadside assistance service to come collect me. Worst-case scenario, the tires could have rapidly deflated, causing the bike to toss me off at speed.

One of the things I am often asked about is what I carry in my tool and spare parts kits. The answer always varies depending on where I am going, what model motorcycle I am using, and how many miles it has.

My first order of business is to build a good toolkit. This usually means junking much of the original toolkit that comes with the motorcycle, except for the special tools they may provide, such as shock and spring adjusters. I then start replacing what I junked with better quality tools unless the original is of good quality. Then I add those items the motorcycle manufacturer forgot, like needle-nose pliers, wire cutters, vise grips, a hacksaw blade, and tire spoons.

I generally end up with the following tools in my kit:

- 3/8-inch drive socket set
- Two to three screwdrivers
- Allen wrenches as needed
- Two extra-long tire irons/spoons
- Hammer with shortened handle
- Vice-Grips
- Large adjustable wrench for big nuts and bolts
- Set of box-end and open-end wrenches
- Hacksaw blade
- Salvaged miscellaneous tools from the original junked toolkit
- Multipurpose super-knife or other cutting tool
- Spare keys (not locked away but not easily found)

My first order of business is to build a good toolkit.

Once I have my toolkit built, I use it to do routine maintenance on the motorcycle rather than go to my big shop toolbox. This way I learn what I need to add, and what I might have added that either did not work or needed to be changed. For instance, I added a 10-millimeter wrench to one toolkit and used it a couple of times. I found that if I bent the head in the vise by 90 degrees it did a much better job at not stripping the one 10-millimeter bolt for which it was needed. I also added to my BMW kit a piece of wire about the thickness of a coat hanger and 10 inches long, bent at the end. It was ideal for pulling oil filters out of their recessed holes as well as moving gears around in the transmission when the return spring broke. The straight end of the wire has had numerous uses for poking and probing.

After I have my tools assembled I put them in either a plastic water-tight frozen-food container lined with foam rubber or an aftermarket nylon tool wrap container. Then I start working on my spare parts and fix-kit. These are the extras I carry, but they range from motorcycle to motorcycle depending on mileage.

Not everything on the spare parts and fix-kit list is needed for every motorcycle.

When touring Japan on a new BMW R1100 RT, all I carried was the multipurpose tool and a credit card. While touring the United States on a new Harley-Davidson Ultra Classic, besides the credit card and multi-purpose utility knife, all I had was a tire pressure gauge.

On the other hand, while touring South America on an older BMW I carried numerous spare parts. These included a spare clutch plate, which I needed, as did another BMW rider when his also failed. Your list of parts and tools may be different depending on your trip. You may be straying far from the security of telephones,

When touring, I check my tires daily.

repair shops, and other such luxuries. Or your specific model may have a unique part or a common mechanical problem. You should keep these factors in mind while packing a toolkit.

Before starting around the world on a new Kawasaki KLR 650, I began to assemble my spare parts kit. I wanted to carry spare electrical parts such as a coil, ignition black box, and charging system components. A Kawasaki representative asked me why I would bother, saying, "They never go bad." I carried them and he was

My spare parts and fix-kit list includes the following:

- Repair manual
- Air pump
- Tire pressure gauge
- Cable ties, mixed
- Miscellaneous bolts/nuts/washers, unique to the motorcycle
- Safety wire
- Electrical wire, 6 feet
- Duct tape
- Electrical tape
- JB Weld Quik
- Goop household glue
- Super glue
- Various hose clamps
- Heat patch kit (for tube tires)
- Tire repair kit for tubeless tires
- Spare tubes
- Several pieces of inner tube, the largest being 6 inches in diameter
- Lightweight battery jumper cables
- Master link for chain
- Fuses
- Circuit tester (amps)
- Oil filter
- Clutch cable
- Electrical parts known to fail on this model of motorcycle
- Several pair of latex gloves
- Small tube of hand cleaner

I pushed my motorcycle under this fruit stand roof in Panama where I had some shade while I removed the transmission and replaced the clutch. It took the better part of an afternoon and I was unhappy at having to spend my time sweating in the 100-degree humidity, but I had all the tools and parts to happily make the repair, plus the knowledge to do it. When I came to the point where a good BMW mechanic would suggest using special BMW grease for the clutch splines, I substituted petroleum jelly, which I did have.

A global touring rider spent his afternoon in a campground in France sorting out electrical gremlins. Fortunately, he was carrying all the tools and electrical parts he would need to sort out his problem and the bike's electrical systems were simple enough to figure out.

An oasis in Africa, the BMW importer in the Republic of South Africa. Many BMW riders touring this part of the world stop in just to feel the security of their spare-parts safety net. There is a dealer network in South Africa and Namibia, but once out of those countries your repairs and maintenance are on your own.

right. However, if you operate on Murphy's Law No. 4 of Motorcycle Touring that says, "What you have is not what you will need," I was actually eliminating problem areas.

One of the best tools you can carry in your toolkit is the club directory specific to your brand and make of motorcycle. These clubs range from the Harley Owners Group to model-specific clubs like the Airhead Beemers Club that is specific to air-cooled BMW models. These clubs provide members with directories of contacts for fellow members who are willing to aid and assist other members with everything from spare rooms, workshops with tools, or coming to collect broken bikes and members on the road. I belong to several of these groups and have found much needed help as well as made new friends several times while touring. These directories are like tools in my toolkit.

Along with the clubs are the numerous Internet groups that you can join not only to help you prepare for your tour but also to provide assistance if you're broken on the road. While they require other tools like a

Not all motorcycle repair shops have a motorcycle repair sign hanging out front. This is a secret repair spot on the Dalton Highway just below the Arctic Circle, behind the Hot Spot Café. Here I was able to change a tire, and the owner took a hammer to a sheet of metal and made a replacement top for an aluminum pannier. I suspect a valve job could be done and a bent wheel straightened too.

laptop computer to make contact, or a cell phone, each can be looked at as an additional tool in your personal toolbox.

When I decided to prepare a Kawasaki KLR 650 for a ride around the globe, I knew little about the motorcycle other than the price was reasonable. I joined an Internet group sponsored by the *Dual Sport News* magazine that was specific to KLRs and asked for the help of interested members. Several agreed to assist me in not only preparing the motorcycle, but also to serve as my "safety net" if I needed help while on my global ride. They were like tools in my toolbox, and I was thankful for their support.

One of the best tools you can carry in your toolkit is the club directory specific to your brand and make of motorcycle.

While touring, most of us are on a schedule. To help keep on that schedule and have routine maintenance performed on your motorcycle through a dealer, schedule your service in advance. If you are planning on

taking a tour of Alaska in July, the peak month for motorcyclists passing through, it is best to call ahead to the shop you want to make the repairs and schedule an appointment. Several days before arriving call again and confirm your appointment. This gives them time to ensure they have the parts and time to do the work you need. It is unrealistic to think they

A motorcycle repair shop in Hanoi, Vietnam. It was amazing to see what these mechanics could do with a hammer, screwdrivers, and pliers. I watched them do a transmission rebuild in less than two hours on a Minsk. There were no Harley repair shops in Hanoi, but my guess is these guys could do a Harley transmission as well as some shade tree mechanics I have met in the United States.

Pick a safe place to make repairs and try to get well off the highway so that you aren't a road hazard or possibly a speed bump, especially at night. I thought I had a secure place outside my motel room. When I went inside for a drink of water a kid ran up and grabbed a handful of my tools, then took off running. I got about half the tools back when they were dropped as I chased him.

All smiles and fun at the Yukon River crossing, these two riders were enjoying their adventure to the Arctic Ocean. A day later the smiles were gone when a flat rear tire resulted in a cut sidewall that was not repairable. The last I heard they were sitting beside the road swatting mosquitoes waiting for a replacement tire to be trucked up from Fairbanks, nearly 500 miles away.

can easily shuffle you in for service during these peak periods, and you may find yourself having to forego the service to keep to your schedule or waiting several days.

The other option is to try and find a place where you can do the work yourself, like change the oil or a tire. If you bring your own oil or tire with you, you will often find places like this much quicker than your brand-specific dealer. You also may find this a way to make new friends along the way because they are often motorheads like yourself and interested in hearing about your tour.

Making repairs on the road has taught me some lessons:

• A leaking tire needs to be fixed or replaced immediately. It does not get well by repeatedly adding air or flat-fix goop.

• If someone offers to give your battery a charge from his or her car or truck, disconnect your battery, especially when your bike has an expensive computer-operated system. The same holds true when having electrical welding done on your bike.

• Engine and transmission additives to swell leaking seals and gaskets are a short-term fix that may cause greater problems because the additives swell more than the one leaking, sometimes requiring a full seal/gasket replacement in a transmission or engine. Oil is cheaper than an engine or transmission overhaul, so you may be far better off just adding oil.

• A duct-tape fix is never a long-term repair.

• When seeing flecks of metal in the oil when changing it, do not assume or hope the cause will go away.

• Water in your oil does not come from condensation. It is a sign of a serious problem that will not get better unless there is a serious repair.

• While riding and hearing a new clicking noise, do not assume it will go away safely or inexpensively. Prayers and hope will seldom help either. Find the cause and repair it.

• When repairing a tire, rub your hand around the inside looking not only for what caused the puncture but other protrusions or foreign objects.

• After plugging a holed tubeless tire with a plug, make immediate plans to replace the tire. The plug is an emergency fix to get you off the road, not a way for you to keep using the tire until it is worn out or you finish your trip. Plugs can come out or leak.

• If you have a flat tire and no way to get it to hold air for you to get off the road to the safety of a nearby town or repair point, fill the flattened tire with clothes like your jeans, T-shirts, and underwear. If you ride slowly the fix can get you to safety. Some off-road tires now come with a similar synthetic "liner."

• If setting the gas tank on the ground while doing repairs, check the opening at the bottom of the petcock to make sure no blockage from dirt will restrict the flow of gas when you put it back on the motorcycle.

While touring the Laos/Thailand border along the Mekong River, my Yamaha Tenere had been carrying me along on a blissful day until it started to misfire. Ignoring the 90 percent electrical rule for most common problems, I drained the carburetor and watched as water came out. Water was in lowest part of my gas tank, an accumulation from two or three years of bad gas. I limped into town and emptied the gas tank, topped it off with fresh gas, and the Yamaha happily carried me away.

It can be a long walk back to town when you can't make repairs on your own. One of the biggest questions is whether to leave the bike unguarded, wait for help to come along, or send out for help. Sending your riding pal for help is another option, unless he is afraid to travel alone or gets lost easily. If available, a good motorcycle roadside assistance policy is a wise investment.

Thinking outside of the box is an important way to deal with repairs on the road. Rather than think that the only solution to your repair is going to be in the womb of your brand-specific dealer's workshop, try to think of other ways the problem can be solved. A traveler across Russia had broken several spokes in his rear wheel. Frustrated by the side of the road in Siberia, his in-the-box form of thinking was wondering how he was going to have some new spokes for his BMW flown in to the end of the world.

When I stopped and asked him if he needed help, he said I could help him only if I could figure out a way to get spokes from Germany or if I was carrying some with me.

I looked at his broken spokes and asked him if he had thought about carefully riding into the next village, about 4 miles away, to see about getting them welded. He looked at me like I was telling him there would be a BMW mechanic there, something totally unbelievable. I told him every town in Russia, no matter how small, would have someone who knew how to weld. If we could find the welder we could weld his broken spokes back together and he could be on his way. Later that day the BMW rider was all smiles as he rode out of town. While the welding job was not the prescribed BMW factory-recommended repair, nor the prettiest, it was functional.

A motorcyclist experienced a rear drive seal failure in Deadhorse, Alaska, about as far as he could get from an authorized BMW dealer to do the warranty work in the United States. Towing his motorcycle back down to Anchorage was going to run nearly $2,000! Instead, he thought outside of the box. He went to the small local airport and found an air cargo company that would crate the motorcycle and fly it to Anchorage for $600. It would go almost immediately instead of waiting several days for a tow truck and trailer. A day later both he and his motorcycle were flown to Anchorage, a new seal was installed, and he was on his way.

Where to make the repair when broken on the road is another out-of-the-box decision that can save you time, money, and possibly your life. A group was touring

Thinking outside of the box is an important way to deal with repairs on the road.

Europe when rain and a misfiring bike caused them to seek shelter under an overpass. While they were standing around watching the frustrated motorcyclist do electrical checks, a speeding car lost control as it approached them and plowed into the bunch, sadly killing one and seriously hurting several others. Had they been standing off the pavement or on the other side of the metal barrier only one would have been hit.

When I have a breakdown on the road I try to get as far away from the traffic lane as possible, even if that means getting dirty. Car and truck drivers will fixate on you and your broken bike as they approach, curious to see what you are doing. When fixated like that they can mistakenly steer their vehicle toward you, especially in panic situations.

PACKING

RULES FOR PACKING

- 1 Pack it light

- 2 Pack it tight

- 3 Pack it low

- 4 Stay within the manufacturer's recommended GVWR.

Saddlebags and top boxes in Taiwan. The packing on this motorcycle violated one of the basic rules when packing: Keep the weight down low.

Light means keep your load light. Tight means keep it compressed tightly to the motorcycle. Low means low to the ground. And GVWR means gross vehicle weight restriction, or the weight the motorcycle was designed to carry.

CHOOSING YOUR PACKING SYSTEM

Today there are ways to mount a set of saddlebags, whether hard or soft, to any model of motorcycle. Some are manufactured and sold as standard accessories with the motorcycle, others are aftermarket products sold as generic add-ons for one size to fit as many models as possible.

A saddle bag system for a motorcycle can cost as little as a couple of hundred dollars to a whopping $2,000. They are all designed to do the same thing: carry gear. The difference is in their function and form. I have used top-of-the-line saddlebags that leaked worse than the army surplus pack sacks I used before plastic or fiberglass bags came on the scene.

Choosing which form of saddlebag you use is based on what you reasonably can afford, what works best for you, and the

A saddle bag system for a motorcycle can cost as little as a couple of hundred dollars to a whopping $2,000.

"look-right" value you place on one over the other. One of my touring friends thought he was getting the best aluminum panniers he could buy for his BMW GS motorcycle because they were the most expensive. He later drilled holes in the bottom of them because he got tired of having to soak the water out of the bottoms every time it rained. To keep things dry he

Ken Craven came out with a line of fiberglass touring boxes and top boxes. I had a set of these in the early 1970s. They leaked a little in a hard rain and fractured and splintered when your motorcycle fell over, but were the top of the line at the time. I kept my things dry inside by packing everything inside plastic bags.

would have been as well off with a pair of saddlebags that cost half what he paid for the high-end pair. He claimed he did not like the cheaper pair because they looked too "boxy" and were not powder coated like his high-end pair.

One of the advantages to purchasing a saddlebag or carrying system sold with the motorcycle is they are often designed to mold to the contours of the motorcycle. Rather than having squared corners, they are rounded for aerodynamics and possible injury prevention when the rider comes in contact with them. The can also integrate their key systems so that one key opens all the boxes and you do not have to try two or three different ones each time you want to lock or unlock a box. The manufacturer can also make the system more comfortable to the eye, matching the system with the fairing, gas tank, and side panels.

Not all motorcycle manufacturers sell good systems with their motorcycles. One manufacturer sold a saddlebag and mount as an offered accessory for the left side of the motorcycle only. Not only was this breaking Rule No. 4 about balancing, but also the view from the rear of the motorcycle made it one of the ugliest motorcycles ever seen, only its mother could have loved it.

Saddlebags can be either top-loaders or side-loaders. With a top-loader the top either comes completely off or is hinged to allow filling the box from the top. Side-loaders are hinged at the bottom and allow filling from the side. If using a side-loader it is preferable that the box come completely off so that you can lay it on its back and open it like a clamshell for filling. If the bag is firmly affixed to the motorcycle or not easily removed, then a bag liner is the second best way to get in your load. The downside to bag liners is they add to the expense of the bag system, and they take up valuable space inside your bag.

Motorcycle manufacturers were quick to pick-up the idea of selling a complete touring package system or mated accessories. In doing so they were able to match the paint and mold saddlebags and top boxes to their specific brands of motorcycles.
Darwin Homstrom

If you are a BMW owner with this type of BMW saddlebag, an inexpensive anti-loss system is to use the straps from the BMW shipping crates, usually thrown away by the dealer, to secure the saddlebag to the bag mount. These saddlebags were infamous for not arriving with their owner at a next stop.

I prefer top-loading bags to side-loading. With a side-loading bag, unless you have a liner inside, everything inside wants to fall out when opened. This "Winger" (see license plate) had top loaders large enough to take a full-face helmet.

Top boxes have found their way into the hearts of various tourers and come direct from the motorcycle manufacturer or numerous aftermarket suppliers. They are ideal for things you want to get at easily and often serve as a backrest for the pillion. On the downside, they can be too easily loaded with heavy items, violating Rules #1 and #3 about light and low.

Some of the top boxes that are sold with the motorcycle are incredibly strong and well built and have as much space as a military footlocker. To prove the theory that a Harley-Davidson Ultra Classic was so gutless it could not do a wheelie, even with the top box filled with car batteries, I did just that, filled one with batteries. The

theory was true, but what was more amazing was how tough and sturdy the H-D top box was, as well as its mounting system.

WEIGHT AND BALANCE

Rule No. 5 for packing is: Balance your load. This means keeping the weight equal in each saddlebag and equally distributed in each bag, the heavier items lower in each bag. With soft-sided bags, and some leather ones, the low and balanced rules can be disastrous when the weight drops the saddlebag onto a hot exhaust pipe or causes the bag to swing up against one. I once burned a hole in a brand-new leather saddle bag on my 1947 Indian Chief, an expensive hole, by carrying my heavy tools and spare parts in the one that hung over the exhaust pipe. It was expensive not only because of the hole in my new $350 bag, but also because the tools worked their way through the hole while I was riding, tinkling onto the road behind me not loud enough to overcome the noise of my engine and exhaust. Loud pipes did not save the life of my toolkit that afternoon.

I have had several subframes on touring motorcycles break because of the added weight of the saddle bag system when full. My solution to this problem has been to try and triangulate the mounting system such that the main frame supports some of the weight. Often this is in the form of a supporting strut from the base of the mounting system to a main frame foot peg or building a bracket that can connect the strut to the main frame. I have also reinforced the subframe at points where it could break and replaced the original mounting bolts with harder ones.

Sometimes I have purchased just the saddlebags or boxes, and then made my own mounting system because the mounting systems offered either did not fit the motorcycle or were not durable enough to support the weight I would be carrying in them. The cost of the self-designed mounts was sometimes higher than purchasing the off-the-shelf ones, but the trade-off was they did not break and have to be replaced or repaired only to break again.

SECURITY AND THEFT PREVENTION

Of all the plastic or molded saddlebags and top boxes, none are theft proof. While we foolishly think the locks on the boxes will

The top boxes on the back of motorcycles seem to get bigger and bigger. This top box on a Goldwing was large enough to easily hold two full helmets with room left over. The tip is to pack heavy items low to keep the center of gravity low and prevent the top box mounts from breaking.

The Harley-Davidson Ultra Classic had a massive top box, large enough to hold my tent, inflatable air mattress, and sleeping bag. When packed there was room left for gloves, a jacket, and walking shoes.

Everything heavy on my Enfield touring bike went in the boxes. What stayed up high were lightweight and bulky items like my sleeping bag, electric vest, and clothing. In the tank bag I carried my cameras and film, where they were easily accessible and away from engine and exhaust heat.

Balance is another rule to packing, trying to keep equal weight on each side of the motorcycle. Common sense taught me not to carry heavy items in one side and light in the other. Too much weight in either bag can easily break the mounting bracket to the frame or the frame itself. When in doubt, reinforce the frame and the brackets.

keep a thief out, imagine how quickly a crow bar could pry a top or side open. In most situations it would take less than 10 seconds. The tip here is to never leave anything valuable locked inside. It is better to empty the bags and boxes at night and leave them open and unlocked, that way the thief will not hurt them by prying them open in the parking lot outside your motel room.

The next step up for security and functionality are metal panniers or boxes. Some self-made ones are modified steel ammunition boxes from an army-navy surplus store mounted to existing or modified mounting systems. While these are rugged and water tight, because they are steel they are heavy and their size often makes them too wide to meet the 1-meter rule.

Aluminum is the choice of nearly all the metal pannier manufacturers, being more pliable and lighter than steel. These systems can range in price from a couple of hundred dollars for thin-fsided sets to nearly $1,600 for the yuppie upwardly mobile options. However, while most are waterproof, none are theft proof.

While traveling to Alaska, a BMW rider had installed the most expensive aluminum panniers but found they were not theft-proof when he lost all of his camping gear in the dark hours of night while the bike was parked in front of his motel room. The thief had quietly pried both tops off using little more than a large screwdriver.

When you have your carrying system mounted and locked on your motorcycle, stand back, look at it, and try to imagine how to get into the boxes if they were locked, not worrying about scratching paint or breaking plastic. Some Freon sprayed on a lock and rapidly hit with a hammer is a trick some thieves also use on steering wheel "anti-theft" bars, as easily done to locks on saddle-bags. To pry the tops off of several well-known aluminum panniers, it can be swiftly and quietly done with a wonderbar or crow bar. Remember, while aluminum is light, it is also pliable. Most of the locking systems that come with aluminum panniers are neither complicated nor durable, they just take a little longer to break than those installed on the plastic boxes or trunks.

One of the advantages to the basic square aluminum pannier is the ease of loading versus trying to work things like laptop computers, bulky shaving kits, and camera cases into contoured boxes. I also like to stay away from multi-angle cut panniers seeing each additional weld as a potential crack.

While some people opt for a large aluminum top box on the back of the motorcycle, I prefer to stack what I need in soft-sided waterproof bags that I can take off and carry into my tent or room for the night, leaving the rear luggage rack empty. The soft-sided waterproof bags, like the Dry Bags offered by Aerostich, are less expensive than an aluminum top box, and weigh far less, thereby meeting Rule No. 1 of keeping things on the back of the motorcycle light.

I have lost several saddlebags off the back of my motorcycle, usually because of attachment failures.

I have lost several saddlebags off the back of my motorcycle, usually because of attachment failures. Once a plastic Krauser saddlebag worked itself loose from the back bracket and fell onto the pavement of Interstate 70 around 10 p.m. I was following a truck that was passing another truck and heard nothing. My riding pal behind me said he felt it fly past his head. It had caught on something and flipped into the air, head high. He said he then noticed it was missing from the back of my motorcycle and raced up to wave me over.

We stopped and he yelled that my high-quality German accessory had nearly taken his head off at 75 miles per hour about a mile back. In my mind I could easily imagine it doing that. I could also imagine my expensive camera inside being road kill, along with the bag. We worked our way back and found the bag 100 percent together lying on the far-left yellow line unscathed, except for some scratches on the back and on one side. Twelve years later it was still mounted on one of my BMW touring bikes, although with better mounting screws and a security strap around the whole bag to hold it tight against the mounting frame.

One of the downsides to the larger, sturdier aluminum carrying systems is the tendency to fill them with more weight and gear than you would the plastic lightweight systems. I once had a client who collected rocks as we toured Alaska. The weight eventually broke the mounting frame, not the aluminum pannier. Had he been filling his factory-offered plastic boxes, I suspect the plastic mount would have snapped before the frame would have.

I once had a Touratech aluminum pannier fall off in heavy traffic on an interstate. I did not realize it was gone until I reached my next stop, 5 miles away. I eventually found it, nearly flattened, with the bottom on one side of the six lanes and the top on the other. The camera inside the bottom was still working. Had the box been plastic I would have had plastic and camera pieces everywhere. I have also often wondered what the car or truck that hit the Touratech box looked like. When people ask me about this brand I say, "Tough stuff. I would not want to run over one with a car." The reason it fell off? Pilot error. I had not retightened the mounting bolts after taking it off and re-installing it.

One of my globe-trotting friends installed on the back of his BMW the biggest set of aluminum panniers he could buy before starting off on a world tour. Before leaving he sent a photo of them and asked what I thought. I kindly wrote back saying, "They look sort of big." Given all the electronic gizmos and gadgets he was

Aluminum panniers or carrying systems came to the United States from Europe. They can be lightweight, sturdy, and need little to no maintenance. Or they can be heavy, crack, and require constant attention. It all depends on how well-made they are. My favorite panniers are a basic box with as few welds as possible made of 2-millimeter-thick aluminum.

One advantage of a factory-built touring rig is that the luggage is part of the motorcycle's original design, and not added as an afterthought.
Darwin Holmstrom

carrying I thought he probably had about 50 pounds worth of gear in each one.

What he forgot to take into consideration was because they were so large, they hung low to the ground. That was in accordance with the rule of keeping weight low. However, they were so low that while he was paddling through some sand in Africa his heel was caught under one and it snapped his 72-year-old leg above the ankle like a toothpick. He got rid of the big boxes in favor of smaller ones.

OTHER ACCESSORIES

Tank panniers are small bags that hang over the gas tank. They come in several sizes and some are waterproof. I like them on motorcycles without fairings because they can carry weight forward on the motorcycle and down low. I never carry things like tools or hard objects in them that could hurt my knees if I were to hit them.

I once attended a motorcycle rally and saw that a seminar presenter promised to tell attendees why he, as a noted traveler and author, did not like tank bags. I decided there would be little I would learn from this expert if he did not know enough to like tank bags, so I passed on his presentation. Later I was told he did not mention tank bags until his seminar was over, and only then when someone in the audience asked him why he did not like them. He answered that he actually did like tank bags and only made that statement to attract people to his seminar.

All of my touring motorcycles have tank bags. I started with them when Harro (a German company) made one monster bag (44 liters, or 10 gallons) that loosely fit many different motorcycles. Theirs, the Elephantboy, had a plastic map cover on top, soft foam on the bottom, and a rain cover to keep things dry. The shell was made with stiff rubber and canvas. They were perfect for moving some weight forward and lower rather than stacking it on the back. On the downside, they were expensive and flopped around because they did not form fit to the gas tank.

While there are a number of tank bags offered in various designs, I prefer those that strap onto the gas tank and are contoured to my specific gas tank shape. The magnetic ones come off too easily. I also like the ones with several pockets, adjustable levels for more or less gear inside, and are waterproof or come with a waterproof cover. I have found some of the aftermarket tank bags are more sturdy and functional (zippers do not break or tear) than the more expensive bags offered by the motorcycle manufacturers. This is quite simply because tank bag manufacturers are in the business to make tank bags, whereas motorcycle manufacturers are in the business to make motorcycles and tank bags are a sideline.

A thinker designs the Wolfman tank bags. Company owner Eric Hougan takes another tank bag or one of his own, studies it, then asks himself how he can make it better. His bags keep getting better and better, and I marvel at the different generations.

I use my tank bags to carry everything from snacks to my cameras, spare gloves to glasses, maps, guidebooks, multipurpose tools, and a tire pressure gauge. The pitfall I sometimes fall into is putting so much heavy gear in the tank bag so that it can become

I use my tank bags to carry everything from snacks to my cameras, spare gloves to glasses, maps, guidebooks, multipurpose tools, and a tire pressure gauge.

top heavy and unwieldy when trying to remove it to get to the gas cap or while trying to make tight turns or riding off-road. I also like a tank bag that is quickly and easily detachable so I can carry it with me when leaving the bike unattended.

Besides being a perfect place to carry a map for reading while driving, I write notes on the clear plastic cover with a dark magic marker, not one of the permanent inked ones but one of the erasable kinds. I can make notes while riding or write directions,

Some manufacturers offer saddlebag liners to facilitate loading and unloading side-opening saddlebags.
Darwin Holmstrom

Cruiser-style touring motorcycles sacrifice some comfort and luggage capacity for stylistic reasons, but in return they have lower centers of gravity and more centralized masses, enhancing handling.
Darwin Holmstrom

Touratech aluminum panniers from Germany are a favorite for European touring motorcyclists. A basic square box with a simple mounting system, they are rugged and found on touring motorcycles at the ends of the earth.

TANK PANNIERS

Definition: Small bags that hang over the gas tank.

Touratech, a German company, designed a left pannier smaller than the right side to account for the upswept muffler on the BMW GS model. The mounting system pulled the boxes close enough together to meet the 1-meter rule and is one reason they have been so popular.

to be ridden in a different section of the lane. While the trailer, like a sidecar, can add additional storage space, it moves riding the motorcycle into another category, that of touring with a trailer.

HOW MUCH?

I once invited a lady friend who was a model to spend some weeks camping and touring the Alps by motorcycle. We bought her a leather riding suit, boots, gloves, and helmet. For wet weather we bought a rubberized rain suit that I told her would go

Carrying gear with trailers changes the motorcycle into something between a car and a motorcycle, a hybrid.

then wipe them off with a towel or cloth. I do not think the designers made their covers for this kind of chemical, but more plastic covers have died or cracked from time and sun than from dark pen markings.

Carrying gear with trailers changes the motorcycle into something between a car and a motorcycle, a hybrid. Not only does the motorcycle steer differently, it also needs

in her saddlebag, along with her other clothes and personal items. I showed her a saddlebag before leaving home so she would have some idea of how much space she would have.

When she arrived in Munich she had two large suitcases. As I lugged them to our hotel room I told her we might have to leave

some of the things inside at the hotel along with the two bags. She said, "But I need everything I brought." To this I answered we would have to see what she had inside.

In the hotel we opened her bags and started to sort through them. Besides her riding boots there were two pairs of running shoes, which she informed me were not both for running. One pair was for walking, like at night.

There was also an assortment of electrical units and two shoe-sized boxes, one for jewelry and one for fingernail work. When I told her we would have to leave these items she started to cry. I calmed her down by saying we'd make room for as much as we could take.

I brought her one saddlebag to the room

I use my tank bags to carry everything from snacks to my cameras, spare gloves to glasses, maps, guidebooks, multipurpose tools, and a tire pressure gauge.

and opened it on the floor. It was a side loader from BMW, so it opened like a clamshell. I put her rain suit in it, then told her to fill the rest of it with what would fit. In the meantime I told her I was going to go downstairs to the *biergarten* to have a beer.

I had two or three beers, giving her nearly an hour to make the hard decisions before returning to the room. There in the middle of the floor was a pile on top of each side of the box nearly a foot and one half high! Everything was neatly folded and stacked, but there was no way the saddlebag would fold shut. At least 75 percent of the pile would have to be removed. When I told her she had done a fine job, but most of it still needed to be left behind, the tears and sobs came again, this time louder and heavier than before.

Again I calmed her, telling her we would

go through the pile and see if we could not somehow make things fit. We agreed to put aside one of the two sweaters, then the bulky jogging suit. As I was digging through the pile I discovered a pair of black stiletto patent leather shoes. As I held them up and asked her what she needed them for she smiled and dug into the remaining pile. She came up with a black lace teddy and said, "The shoes go with this," as she held it up to her body. I thought for a few

Luggage racks bolted to top-box covers are best used for decorative purposes since loads heavier than the Road Runner can stress the top box cover, causing cracks in the plastic. *Darwin Holmstrom*

Need more carrying capacity than saddlebags and a top box? Add a trailer. I once asked a trailer-pulling motorcyclist parked at a motel what he carried in the trailer if it wasn't filled with camping gear. He said he and his wife would leave home with the trailer empty and fill it with souvenirs as they toured.

PACKING LIGHT

One-third of one of my saddlebags is usually full of tools and spare parts. I carry enough clothing to go for two to three weeks without having to stop and find a laundry (I wash underwear in hotel rooms from time to time) and have two sets of clothes, one for riding and one for when I am not riding.

seconds, then said, "I think I know where they both can go." The shoes were carefully packed each morning inside of my rolled up sleeping bag, the teddy in hers. While they were not needed as part of our camping or riding gear, both were appreciated when worn.

Just how much gear is right for a motorcycle tour varies significantly from one rider to the next. My credit card touring buddies tour with little more than their plastic, a cell phone, and a change of clothes. When they need clean socks they stop and buy some, along with shorts and shirts. If they break down they call a towing service on their cell phone, or wait for the chase truck running sweep to collect them, or the tour mechanic inside to make the needed repairs. Besides their credit cards they need little more than a glasses case for their Ray-Ban sunglasses and a pocket for their cell phone.

On the other hand, someone like myself, who tours around the world without a safety net and on a limited budget, must carry considerably more. One-third of one of my saddlebags is usually full of tools and spare parts. I carry enough clothing to go for two to three

weeks without having to stop and find a laundry (I wash underwear in hotel rooms from time to time) and have two sets of clothes, one for riding and one for when I am not riding.

TEST RIDES

Before I leave on a tour I load my motorcycle and make a test ride. Not only am I checking the motorcycle and changes I may have made to it, but I am also checking to see how my weight is distributed. If, when I take my hands off the handlebars at any speed, the front end wants to wobble, I stop and move weight from the back of the motorcycle up high to more forward and lower.

Before I leave on a tour

I load my motorcycle and

make a test ride.

I carefully check my tie-down systems. Some people favor straps, I do not. I find them cumbersome and awkward to work with. Others favor cargo nets, which I hate.

I spend more time each day unhooking and untangling them from themselves than they're worth. While cargo nets are about the only way to safely secure a spare helmet on the back of a motorcycle I seldom carry a spare helmet. What I do favor are heavy-duty bungee cords, the kind with plastic-coated hooks to protect paint. If they are too long to secure their load tightly I either cut them and make them shorter or tie knots in the end to take up the slack.

One of my lady touring acquaintances who was new to motorcycling told me she hated bungee cords and would only use heavy tie-down straps, the kind used to tie motorcycles down to pallets or onto trailers. I asked her why she would opt to carry so much weight in tie downs over the lighter and superior bungee cords. Her explanation was that she had not secured a bungee securely once and it had come loose and hit her in the face. I said, "So, you learned how to make sure they don't come loose after that. So what else is wrong with them?" She stared at me like I was from outer space, then I realized why. Her learning curve for

securing bungee cords had not flattened out after the first whack in the face. The last I saw of her she was still strapping her gear on with 6-foot lengths of bike tie downs.

After my test I make a list of what I carried.

After my test I make a list of what I carried. My A column includes those things I absolutely must carry, like tools, air pump, helmet, jacket, boots, gloves, raingear, cameras, change of clothing, prescription drugs, and camping equipment if I am sleeping and eating outside. My B list is for those things I use or could purchase along the way if needed, but could manage without. On this list goes my walking around shoes, extra set of glasses, flashlight, laundry soap, sewing kit, reading material, and more changes of clothes. My last list is the C list, or that gear that I carried and never used or could easily live without but was nice to have. On this list goes the CD or tape player, CDs or tapes, spare batteries,

TANK BAGS AND WEIGHT

Do not store heavy items in your tank bag. Besides going against the Golden Rule No. 3 of keeping your center of gravity low, weight in the tank bag causes it to flop around, possibly interfering with steering when it wedges itself between the handlebars and the gas tank.

The trailer attached to this touring bike was as big as my whole motorcycle (in the background) and, if needed, could probably carry it.

While trikes made from motorcycles might look like the most comfortable touring rigs on the planet, their unstable handling makes them somewhat less desirable. A single-tracked vehicle was never meant to have more than two wheels. *Darwin Holmstrom*

There is no specific list of what you **must** *pack for your tour.*

umbrella, GPS, cell phone, inflatable air mattress, jacket, second pair of pants, dress shirt, and numerous other gadgets and gizmos. After I get my motorcycle loaded with the A and B list I start to carefully inspect my C list for what I will need and what I can manage without. For a long hard tour the C list gets left behind. If I am taking a short tour and have the capacity, I will drag along the C list.

There is no specific list of what you must pack for your tour. While my friends happily tour behind a guide with a chase truck following them on perfectly smooth roads along the coast of Brazil, I am equally happy surviving solo on the mud tracks of the Brazilian jungle knowing if my motorcycle or I break down, I have to have with me what I need to survive. The real answer is to take what makes you feel comfortable.

The real answer is to take what makes you feel comfortable.

Whew! That's what I said when I saw this fully loaded BMW. While it did not have the biggest carrying system of saddlebags and tank bags I had seen in the world, the bag on the back was. I wondered what was in that large red bag? Maybe a tent big enough for a family, and hopefully not a spare engine.

PACKING A FIRST-AID KIT

By Darwin Holmstrom

Whenever you ride a motorcycle, you should carry a first-aid kit. You can purchase a pre-packaged first-aid kit, but you should add some items to address problems specific to motorcycling.

Most pre-packaged first-aid kits contain the following items (if not, add them):
- Adhesive tape
- Antiseptic ointment
- Antiseptic towlettes
- Band-Aids (assorted sizes)
- Gauze pads and roller gauze (assorted sizes)
- Scissors and tweezers
- Triangular bandage
- Disposable gloves

Supplemental items to add to a commercially-supplied first-aid kit:
- Several 30-inch-by-30-inch unbleached muslin triangle bandages/slings
- Small EMT shears or heavy-duty scissors capable of cutting boot leather

The adhesive tape , towelettes, and antiseptic ointment should suffice for extremely minor injuries. In the event of a serious injury, your focus should be on stopping the bleeding until it can be treated by a medical professional. You will want to supplement the Band-Aids, gauze pads, and roller gauze supplied in the kit. Purchase enough unbleached muslin from a sewing supplies store to make several 30-inch-by-30-inch triangle bandages and you'll be prepared for nearly any survivable injury. These can also be used to make slings for broken arms.

The first step towards treating an injury is finding the injury, which can mean cutting off an injured rider's leather or textile riding gear. You'll want to include a pair of small EMT shears, or at least a pair of scissors rugged enough to cut off a competition-weight leather jacket or a pair of leather riding boots.

Other useful items to include in your kit:
- Tampons: Ask any EMT and he or she will tell you that tampons are one of the most useful tools available for stemming the flow of blood (maxi pads also come in quite handy for this purpose).
- Imodium AD, especially when traveling outside the United States or Canada: I don't think I need to draw you a picture here.
- Electrolyte tablets: Heat stroke can be deadly.
- An Ace Bandage, or other type of elastic bandage: Sometimes you'll need to keep a sprained or broken bone in place long enough to get help, even when traveling in populated regions.
- Razor knife or scalpel: For those quick roadside tracheotomies.

Chapter 5

GIZMOS AND GADGETS

WHAT YOU WILL LEARN

- Choosing accessories for safety, comfort, and appearance

- Weighing the costs and benefits of certain accessories

- What you NEED versus what's nice to have... or downright necessary

This Harley-Davidson had enough gadgets behind the fairing to attract the general passerby. Especially interesting were the small leather pocketbook-like pouches attached to the windscreen. I wondered how often the owner had come back to his bike to find they had been opened by inquiring minds looking for small change, tire gauges, or more.

America is the land of touring motorcycle gizmos and gadgets. Nowhere else in the world are there more accessories and touring aids available to the touring motorcyclist as there are in the United States. Not only are they available, but Americans have the disposable income to purchase them.

I was once looking at one of my buddy's touring motorcycles that had enough electronic gizmos wired into it as the cockpit of a Boeing 747. I jokingly commented that he had more money tied up in his gizmos and gadgets than he did in the bike. He frowned and snapped back, "That's not funny." I suppose it wasn't when you consider he had started with a $20,000 motorcycle.

Motorcyclists are generally recognized as being individualists, and as such we like to customize or individualize our motorcycles to make them stand apart from the one our neighbor just bought. We can do it with as little as a deer whistle glued on the front fender or a

machete strapped to one of the front fork legs. Either way, we have added a gizmo or gadget that looks like it has some application. Neither one aids in our touring, however.

America is the land of touring motorcycle gizmos and gadgets.

I try to keep my motorcycle gadget- and gizmo-free. Not only are many of these add-ons only of marginal use, but they can heavily attack my budget. For instance, a sound system or GPS can easily cost me half a month's travel budget. The gizmos and gadgets can also grow legs and walk away from the bike when I am not looking or watching them carefully. I also dislike having to remove them at night when my bike is parked away from the safety of my home, or when I have to ride in the rain.

This motorcycle had a mix of simple and complex gadgets and gizmos, enough to keep the pilot occupied while riding. For those long stretches of boring interstate highways across America, the addition of gizmos and gadgets can break up the monotony of thousands of miles of emptiness.

A favorite gizmo for travelers these days is a laptop computer, the riders claiming they need to connect with the Internet. An alternative to lugging around the expensive weight is to stop at an Internet café, like this one in Germany.

HI-TECH VS. LO-TECH

One simple accessory I have learned to appreciate is a pair of earplugs. Not only do they reduce wind and traffic noise, but I know I grow fatigued slower when I ride with them than without. Earplugs reduce aural fatigue and after using them for a while I have noticed that when I do not have them in my ears I miss them. I have a custom set for plugging into a sound system, but more often I use the cheap disposable ones because I do not have to deal with the wires and where to put the tether when I am not listening to music or my radar detector.

One simple accessory I have learned to appreciate is a pair of earplugs.

Radar jammers and detectors give the rider a false sense of security. If you are not speeding you will need neither. If you decided to risk the hit to your driver's license and insurance rates by exceeding the speed limit, the detector might save you but the jammer, which is illegal, is junk.

The problem with radar detectors is that by the time they alert you, you've already been seen and quite possibly your speed has been recorded if you are out front. For instance, if you're riding across the wide open spaces of Wyoming all alone and your detector lights up there is a good chance your speed has been recorded by the officer coming the opposite direction. Slowing down to the speed limit is useless because you have already been tagged.

GPS SYSTEMS

The Touratech company once loaned me a motorcycle for a short tour. It was a display model that featured many of their aftermarket options, some I never did figure out how to work. For instance, it came with a GPS mounted on one of the manufactured handlebar mounts. Oddly, the screen was frozen "on" and I could not find a way to shut it off. I was riding on autobahns across Europe that I knew from my many previous trips, so I did not even bother with a map. However, because the GPS was perched there in plain sight I would carefully remove it at night or when I was away from the motorcycle and carry it with me.

When I returned the motorcycle it was raining, so I had the GPS in my coat pocket protecting it. I handed it to the owner and told him there was something wrong with it because the screen had been frozen "on" since I had left. He took it, looked at me, then started to laugh. He explained to me that he was laughing because while I had been carefully protecting the GPS from rain or theft each night, it had not needed such attention. It was a display model, was gutless inside, and the map frozen on the screen was pasted to the inside of the screen. Then I had to laugh with him, telling him I had wondered about the unit a little bit because the map on the screen was from somewhere in the United States and not Europe.

I once attended a seminar that was given by Nick Sanders to a group of Triumph motorcycle enthusiasts in England. Nick had established he was the fastest man to travel around the world on a motorcycle, a Triumph, and the group was interested in hearing about the ride and some of his experiences. At the end of his presentation one of the owners asked Nick what kind of GPS he had used on his record-setting ride of just under 32 days. Nick answered he did not use one. A gasp went up from the gathered crowd. He then sent them further into shock by adding that he did not even use a map.

Nick went on to explain that he had toured the world before, twice by bicycle and once on a slow Royal Enfield, so he felt he did not need electronic gadgetry to show him roads he had already seen. He also explained that he wanted to keep his wiring system and motorcycle electrics as simple as possible to avert having any electrical problems on his highly publicized and expensively promoted timed tour of the world.

I was once arguing with a touring guru about whether or not a GPS was a necessary gadget for motorcycle touring. He made a strong case, saying having one could keep a motorcyclist from getting lost, for instance, in the deserts of Africa. He went on to point out the maps of the African desert often did not show way points for water holes or where sand tracks turned off and petered out or when gas could be found, while coordinates given by others for these places could save your life by getting you there with your GPS. I had to agree. Knowing where not to go, or where to find water and gas would be important. Then I asked him how often had he toured the deserts of Africa, or if he ever planned to. "Never" was his answer, but he came back at me with what he thought would be his own debate finisher by asking me how many times I had carried a GPS while traveling in the deserts of Africa, knowing I had been there more than once. My answer was like his, "Never."

Keeping it simple, this motorcycle's owner had only added a couple of gadgets. Left alone in a parking lot they might stay attached and might not. I have lost less-valuable items glued to my fairing, like a cheap plastic watch, while parked in front of some upscale hotels.

I was once asked to join a touring group for a day. They all had CB radios and wanted to know what my handle was. I told them I didn't have one, or a CB. They were astonished and asked how I could ride in a group without a CB. My answer was simple: I usually don't ride in groups.

Radar jammers and detectors give the rider a false sense of security.

Where the radar detector can be useful is when it goes off and you were speeding, lucky enough not to be in the front position alone but preparing to pass, or nearly out in front. It gives you a wake up call to slow down and duck back into traffic until the unit quiets down and you have passed the danger zone.

Long distance riders who are in a hurry or are trying to meet a rally schedule enjoy radar detectors because most know they are going to be speeding. If you are not going to be speeding then, logically, you will not need a radar detector unless you argue the noise they make brings you back to attention or wakes you up. If this is the case, you need some rest and not a radar detector.

If you are going to be speeding, then I would suggest a combination of a CB radio with a radar detector is your best bet. If you are listening to the road chatter and your radar detector is working you may well receive advance warning when approaching electronic surveillance. The CB will do you far more good if the officer is using VASCAR or spotter planes to pace you, or if an unmarked pace car has been identified.

One of my favorite gadgets is a throttle lock or cruise control. These come in various forms, but all serve to hold the throttle open at a certain position so that it does not slam shut when you take your hand off. There are many times during my

One of my favorite gadgets is a throttle lock or cruise control.

When packing, I put the laptop computer on my "C" list, something that is nice to have but I can tour without it.

riding day that I want to use my right hand, or both hands, while riding. The throttle slamming closed can be annoying and dangerous if it happens in a curve or on a wet or icy section of road.

The age of computers has created such a dependence on them, some tourers insist they are a necessary item on their touring list. I managed quite well on four rides around the world without one. They are handy, though expensive and heavy. Also, like a camera or a portable CD player, they are easily stolen and subject to water damage. When packing, I put the laptop computer on my "C" list, something that is nice to have but I can tour without it. Some riders are so dependent on their computers that they move them to their A column, the "must-take" items.

I do not write much while touring. I have yet to see a good book ground out on a laptop computer while someone is on the road, but they do make it easier to keep diaries. Personally, I do not see much fun in touring all day then sitting in my tent or room at night pecking out words with a flashlight duct-taped to my head. I leave that work for when I return to my office.

The mapping programs you can purchase for a laptop can help you plan your trip and are fun and often useful. Yet much of that can be done and printed before you

leave and the paper stuffed in your tank bag. Some users of these programs are so tied to them that they plan their toilet stops, something my internal organs have not given over to computer chips.

The more gadgets and gizmos you have on your bike, the more likely you are to become distracted from keeping your eyes on what is in front of you.

While Internet cafés and access points blanket the world, the United States is behind in this category, mostly because in other parts of the world people cannot afford their own personal computer and the cost of Internet access. Where Internet access can be found in the United States, it is often expensive, such as at copy centers. Some of these places charge as much for one hour as it costs for a month of access from your home. If you are an Internet junkie who has to read stock market reports, post-trip diaries, and read or send e-mail daily, then carrying your own equipment with you,

A quality aftermarket saddle is one accessory most touring riders agree is necessary. *Darwin Holmstrom*

An engine case guard is another accessory most touring riders use. In a minor tip-over, such guards prevent crippling damage to engine cases. *Darwin Holmstrom*

awkward and heavy as it may be, may be the trade-off for the money saved.

Cyber cafés can range from plush sound-proof booths to rows of hard plastic stools in front of ancient monitors occupied by video game–playing kids blasting laser guns with joysticks or playing loud music. They are also good places to catch computer viruses if the owners are not keeping their computers clean with the latest firewalls or system protection programs. I do not re-use a disc in my own computer after I have used it in a cyber café. They are cheap enough to throw away compared to what it might cost to have my laptop cleaned after I brought back an infection.

BMW's K1200LT is the motorcycle-touring gizmo and gadget king. If it's not available as an accessory on this bike, you *really* don't need it.

This cup holder gadget made sense until I remembered that while drinking out of a cup and riding, the wind usually sucks the liquid past its intended target and onto my face and glasses.

Safety bars and engine guards have found their way onto almost all of my touring motorcycles.

One of the hottest selling gizmos in the motorcycle market is the GPS. They can range in price from several hundred dollars to $1,500, depending on what comes with it in the way of programs and mounting systems. While there are pros and cons to these neat little computers, they still do not remove the need for paper maps, and as Nick Sanders explained, neither are needed to ride around the world.

One of my sponsors sells a lot of GPS units and says they are like the CB radio, a nice toy, but definitely not needed to tour by motorcycle. Again, like the radar detectors, they are invaluable tools for rally racers or someone trying to beat the clock in a timed event.

I was once traveling with a friend who had a GPS. She would yell at me to let me know how high we were, what the temperature was, how long we had been riding, what our average speed was, and other useless information I had no need for while riding the main road through Sikkum. Once we stopped she yelled over to me that we

were 50 feet from the border, and I pointed to the border fence 50 feet away and said I could see that. When we crossed the Tropic of Capricorn she yelled over to let me know, and I pointed to the large yellow road sign that confirmed her GPS reading.

The more gadgets and gizmos you have on your bike, the more likely you are to become distracted from keeping your eyes on what is in front of you. Rather than have my eyes stuck on the temperature reading or where the best Chinese restaurant is located, I would prefer to have them roving the road or street in front of me for that pothole that could waffle my $600 front wheel or the deer that wants to dart out of the woods. I like the toys, but do not want to put my safety behind being able to tell what the temperature is or how high I am above sea level.

SAFETY AND COMFORT ACCESSORIES

Safety bars and engine guards have found their way onto almost all of my touring motorcycles. Not only do they protect

NICE TOUCHES

Drinking water, soda, or coffee without stopping has several advantages, and drink holders seem to be a good way to keep the drink from spilling. If I must take water or another beverage with me while riding, I prefer it to be from a bladder in my tank bag or on my back. That way I have both hands doing what they should be, managing the handlebars, and not trying to stabilize a cup filled with coffee.

Optional foot pegs give me a way to shift around on the motorcycle while riding. I like them on some touring bikes, but find them to be ugly protrusions on others, catching on everything from my pants to door jambs and painted surfaces. If they stick out farther than the handlebars or saddlebags when folded inward, I do not use them. While not as neat, chromed crash bars or engine protectors can just as easily give me a sitting option.

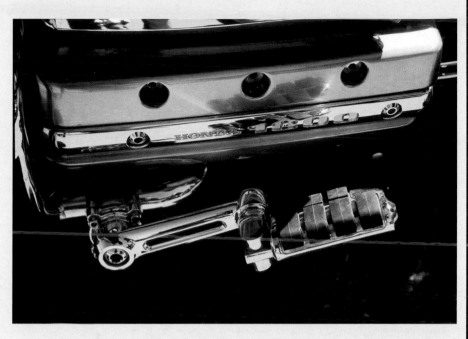

A leg/footrest gadget can allow you to change your riding position. When I first saw this one I thought it was a side stand, but upon inspection I found it was a foot peg that neatly folded out of the way when not in use.

Helmet communicators are fun for short periods, but as I seldom ride with others or a pillion, I find them unnecessary gadgets. When I did use them with a pillion, I found her constant talking to be a distraction. While I listened for cars approaching from the rear or odd engine sounds, I had to filter out what she and her mother had talked about the evening before or questions about passing landmarks I knew nothing about. While some people love them because they can talk back and forth, I find them to be more wires and weight I can ride without.

Heated handgrips are some of the most practical cold-weather gizmos sold for bikes. When cold sets in, these can make a miserable ride less miserable because your hands are warm. Just that small warmth on your body makes your feel much better all over. On the down side, they are more wires and connections, another place for blue smoke to come from when something goes wrong, and on some of my touring motorcycles the electrical system is so marginal to begin with I am inviting a dead battery or overworked charging system.

exposed vulnerable parts like radiators and water pumps in case of a small tip over, they can serve as my alternate foot rests on long, smooth sections of roads.

Adding lights to the motorcycle, front and back, has the obvious advantage of being able to see and be seen more easily. I like more candlepower up front if I can install it without draining my electrical system. My best alternative to this expensive set of gadgets is to try to limit my riding after dark. Since I enter no contests or tours that require nighttime riding, I can

usually plan the route during the daylight hours well enough to be able to park before sunset.

The cell phone is another gadget I can tour without. While some touring riders move this item onto their A list, it is in my C column, a nice gadget to have but not needed.

Spare gas tanks with fuel pumps to transfer gas to the main tank while riding are another neat gizmo; however, the high price of an auxiliary tank and the fact that gasoline is available just about everywhere

A gizmo and gadget vendor had some custom-made touring items for BMW LT motorcycles at a rally. America is undoubtedly the gizmo and gadget capital of the world when it comes to aftermarket items a motorcyclist can add to their motorcycle. While the rest of the world is limited by government regulations or disposable income, America remains the land of plenty.

I like gadgets that contribute to my touring comfort, not those that merely dress up the motorcycle.

within a 200-mile range makes having a 10- to 12-gallon capacity an expensive option. Personally, I do not like sitting on a motorcycle long enough to consume 10 gallons of gas. If my goal is to make my touring comfortable, making use of a $1,000 extra-large gas tank works against my goal. Of course, if I want the macho-man look of the guy whose bladder can toughen out 300 to 500 miles without a stop, then I've got to have the tank to match.

The other downside of the add-on gas tanks is the extra weight, and what it will replace in my list of A and B category items.

The auxiliary gas tank items make my C list, looking better on someone else's motorcycle than mine.

I once seriously considered adding an extra gas tank to a Harley-Davidson that had a pitifully small tank. I would have to start worrying about gas after 75 miles of riding. I spent a lot of time researching larger gas tanks until it suddenly dawned on me that I needed to stop every 75 to 100 miles anyway, so it might as well be for gas. Sitting on top of that Harley-Davidson was like sitting on top of a washing machine with several bowling balls inside. After an

A simple add-on wind deflector can make a long hard day of helmet buffeting into one of riding bliss. If your windscreen is too low to deflect wind at 50 miles per hour over your helmet, an inexpensive option is adding height and not purchasing a whole new screen. The modification may require additional bracing for the original screen to prevent cracking.

hour, hour and a half, my hands, feet, and knees were numb and my insides shook up enough for my kidneys to be screaming STOP! I eventually solved both problems by selling the motorcycle to someone who was quite happy just to ride it around town on the weekends.

I like gadgets that contribute to my touring comfort, not those that merely dress up the motorcycle. For instance, if I can add

> *Piloting a sidecar is as different from riding a motorcycle as riding a motorcycle is from driving a car.*

a minor item like an add-on wind deflector to move the force of the wind off my chest or face shield and around my body I will consider it. I can see no reason to purchase a plastic stick-on fake carbon-fiber gas tank cap cover. It does not contribute to my comfort unless I feel comfortable in giving away $30. I feel much better spending $30 on a wind deflector.

One of my favorite gadgets is a sheepskin or air-filled seat cover. I can move these from one motorcycle to the other, making all my seats more comfortable. I scoffed at them when they were first suggested, dismissing them as something for the riders with office butts, used to sitting on a stuffed chair all day, week after week. After I used one on a particularly ugly BMW seat, I was convinced and started moving it around to my other motorcycles whether their seats were hard or not. The downside to them is they get wet easily and hold water like a sponge. If I see rain looming I pull over and take it off, stuffing it in my tank bag or tank panniers to keep it dry.

One of the largest gadgets you can add to your motorcycle is a sidecar. I have used several of them and found them to be a different way of riding, like having a trailer on the back. You have moved from the category of motorcycle touring to something

else, something between a motorcycle and a car. While you are still wearing your riding gear and sitting on top of a motorcycle, you have changed the vehicle so drastically that few of your training and skills are applicable. Piloting a sidecar is as different from riding a motorcycle as a motorcycle is from driving a car.

Sidecars are fun and I still use one occasionally, but as soon as I am hauling the weight around, trying not to leave it slammed into the back of a car I am passing

A unique gadget was this pair of tank panniers on a BMW. They allowed for the storage of objects such as gloves or inner tubes on top of the tank in a tank bag while lowering the center of gravity and providing a bit of a windscreen for the rider's knees and upper legs.

and manhandling the handlebars, I know I have wandered far from my two-wheel base. There is no doubt you can carry more luggage and gadgets with the extra space a sidecar affords, including the whole family. The one thing I have

Having seen motorcycles touring the world for nearing 40 years, I still see gizmos and gadgets that cause me to scratch my head and wonder "Why?"

noticed about sidecars is that often the girl who was trained by her mother to "never, never, never get on the back of a motor-cycle" will jump into a sidecar without any qualms. For the guy trying to meet girls with his motorcycle, the sidecar can be a valuable gizmo to add.

This stuffed animal attached to the handlebars had a wet day. While I have never been able to determine what function these attachments perform, they must do something because I've seen some as big as a person attached to seats, top boxes, and on top of gas tanks.

This gizmo found on my friend's Kawasaki had a purpose. It was holding the nametag for the motorcycle owner.

Of all the things I have seen added to motorcycles, the stuffed animals have escaped reasoning and explanation. When I have asked owners why they have added them I get a wide range of answers from "My wife [or girlfriend] thinks it is cute" to "It's my mascot" or "It brings me good luck." The stuffed animals do not meet the requirements for my A or B list, and while they fall in the C category, they're near the bottom of that list.

One of my touring friends went a step further than the stuffed animal and packed his dog around with him. The dog rode in an airline pet carrier, one of those large plastic crates with a wire door and mesh windows on the side. I asked the owner if the dog liked riding in the box and he said it had, until the day the box came off the back of the bike at speed on a dirt road. After that day, he always had a little trouble getting the dog to go into the box.

Having seen motorcycles touring the world for nearing 40 years, I still see gizmos and gadgets that cause me to scratch my head and wonder "Why?" One of the oddest was a horse saddle instead of

the motorcycle seat. I grew up and still live around horses and have found sitting on a saddle about as comfortable as sitting on a board. When I asked the bike owner about the saddle he explained it had always been his dream to come to America and be a cowboy, to ride the range on a horse. He said that he had tried to work out a feasible way to see America from a horse but found it to be too slow and not an easy way to get through cities, so he purchased a motorcycle and swapped the seat for his saddle. He said he still felt like he was riding a horse that way.

And then there was the German traveler I heard about who had taken a 1950s-style radio and mounted it on his handlebars in lieu of a windscreen, the knobs and dial facing him. It was high enough to flow the air over his head and gave him some protection from rain. The weight was not much because he had gutted the insides. So I guess if you looked at it from a comfort and practicality standpoint it was functional. If you see him, maybe you can find out the answer to my "Why?"

After touring America for more than 40 years I have yet to find an answer for what function these performed. One suggestion was that they keep the front wheel pointed straight; another was to dry out the owner's boots. I submitted they were there to let the owner know which way was right and left, like turn signals.

Chapter 6

KEEP WARM, DRY, AND COOL

WHAT YOU WILL LEARN

- Strategies for layering your riding gear to stay warm, cool, and dry

- Using additional fairings, windscreens, or other bodywork additions as both a riding/packing accessory and a protection against the elements

- Tips for staying cool and hydrated without sacrificing body protection

A rider in the Nevada desert shows what he thinks is the best way to stay cool.

To get cool you need to get your exposed body out of the direct light of the sun.

A critical element to touring is that the rider be comfortable. This means warm when it is cold, dry when it is wet, and cool when it is hot. What you wear while riding can determine all three of these factors.

Actually, what the above-pictured rider is doing to cool off is working against his goal. A given when the sun is beating down is that it is cooler in the shade. To get cool you need to get your exposed body out of the direct light of the sun. You do not see Bedouins in the Sahara desert walking around nearly naked in the sun. Instead you see them completely covered in breathable flowing garments, from head to toe except for their eyes or face, keeping their bodies out of the direct sunlight. In cases of heat, cold, or moisture, the key is always to avoid exposure. The same applies to you when riding.

KEEPING WARM

As one of the founders of the infamous Elephant Ride, where in early February we would ride our motorcycles over treacherous snow-covered passes in the high Colorado Rocky Mountains, sometimes during below-zero weather and snowstorms, I have learned a few things about staying warm when it is cold. Some of those lessons I have applied when touring Alaska, others when riding as near to Antarctica as I could get.

One of my first lessons was that it was easier to stay warm by bundling-up before getting cold than it was to warm myself up after I got cold. Sometimes when I got cold from riding and stopped to add clothing, I never warmed up.

Another lesson in staying warm is to forget about fashion and form or looking good. Riding in my tight-fitting leather riding gear looks and feels good, but it has found me closely approaching hypothermia several times. The uglier and bulkier riding gear, layered and loose, while it may not look good, does a far better job at keeping me warm. That is because layered and

Leather rider clothing is still popular but has lost ground to textile riding gear. Leather is known to be hot in the summer, not warm in the winter, and like a sponge when it rains. I have several leather riding suits that have been retired, but I do bring them out on nice riding days. I have not done any touring with a leather riding suit in five or six years.

This "crusty" rider in a well-worn Aerostich riding suit claimed that while it looked old and worn the suit still kept him warm and dry.

loose clothing traps warm air in spaces surrounding the body, creating pockets of insulation.

When layering closest to your body, your inner layer, you should use clothing that is made of material that draws moisture away from your body while continuing to insulate when wet. It should also dry quickly. That rules out cotton underwear, long johns, and 99 percent of motorcycle T-shirts. A better choice is inner clothing of varying weights of polypropylene, available through motorcycle specialty retailers like Aerostich/Riderwearhouse (www.aerostich.com) or good outdoor clothing stores. They will have everything from socks and long underwear to glove liners.

The second layer, between your inner and outer layer, should be made of something that retains body heat while at the same time keeps out the cold. There are a wide range of material composites in this category, including compressed polyester fleece and spun synthetic filaments. These are superior to wool because wool absorbs moisture and is slow to dry. Pound for pound, polyester pile or compressed polyester fleece is warmer and thicker. You will notice cotton fails at this layer too, so leave home the long sleeve tees and sweatshirts favoring the name of your favorite brand of motorcycle, or confine them to use in the evening, *après de touring*. Also, rule out

One of the benefits to textile touring clothing is that it's easy to clean. When mine gets a little muddy, like this rider's, I wear it into the shower or wash it off at a car wash when cleaning my motorcycle.

CHEAP WIND AND RAIN HAND PROTECTORS

Hand protectors from wind and rain can be fashioned from two empty plastic soda containers from a mini-mart. Cut off the back 1/4 to 1/3 of a 2-liter bottle and make enough room on the neck to clamp over the handlebars. Duct tape or cable-tie the bottle opening over the handlebars. It will be a flimsy fix, but done right will keep your hands or gloves from direct rain or wind.

those wool socks and sweaters your aunt knitted for you.

The outer layer of your cold-weather riding gear can take several forms. If you can struggle into your form-fitting leathers you will find it cuts the wind, but the tightness will constrict your movement. If it's raining you will want to add an additional waterproof layer on top of your leathers to keep the leather from soaking up the rain. My personal preference is a Gore-Tex outer layer or something made of a similar breathable material. These fabrics allow perspiration to escape while at the same time prevents water from penetrating.

The downside to these types of breathable materials is they allow wind to enter. If I am having an especially cold and wet riding day, I put on my nonporous rain suit over my outer layer. I am careful not to seal the rain suit completely to allow the wind to suck out some of the perspiration buildup from the inside. The rain suit I favor is one that has venting in the armpits and a protected vent in the back. The pants have vents behind the knees and in the upper back.

With the rain suit on, and a pair of warm, waterproof riding boots and waterproof gloves, the only source of heat loss I have left to deal with is from my head. I wear a full-faced helmet that keeps the wind off my head, but like all helmets it has numerous air leaks, justifiably needed

to let perspiration out. The one remaining piece of warm weather gear I add is a non-cotton balaclava that covers my neck and head.

Fully entombed in my cold-weather riding gear I look like the Pillsbury Doughboy rolled in chocolate sprinkles. On the upside, I am warm inside my wrapping.

If it's raining you will want to add an additional waterproof layer on top of your leathers to keep the leather from soaking up the rain.

On all my touring bikes I have installed windscreens and full fairings or they came with factory wind/rain protectors. The benefit of having something in front of me diverting the wind or rain around me is I am able to stay warmer by not being blasted directly. While these protectors are sometimes unwieldy and expensive, the trade-off of staying warm and dry longer is worth it to me. I enjoy riding in the bubble behind the protection and am willing to give-up the "riding in the wind" image in exchange for being warm.

This German rider was ready for anything a Swiss summer day could throw at her on a high pass. Her touring suit was waterproof, yet breathed in the 90-degree heat at lower altitudes. The suit was expensive but provided superior protection over her leather riding suit.

And then there are the times when you start out warm and ride into the cold. Then you will find you have to find a place to pull over and do the getting dressed project, often while hopping around on one foot by the side of the road or in a rest stop.

KEEPING DRY

One touring trick I have learned when I start to get cold is to pull over and suit-up in my raingear. This plastic riding gear keeps the wind from getting at me directly. Even though I wear a full riding suit of Gore-Tex, I still carry a rain suit for times like this. It takes up little space, is relatively inexpensive, and has multiple uses, not only as raingear but also for wind protection.

Keeping out of the rain is the first line of defense in staying dry, and some piece of plastic or a deflector on the front of your motorcycle will help. Whether it is a fairing or windscreen, the purpose is to deflect the wet around you.

One option I have found that works nearly as well as a pricy fairing, and has side benefits, is using an inexpensive combination of a handlebar-mounted windscreen, gas tank panniers, and a tank bag.

Some would rightfully argue that a handlebar-mounted windscreen can affect steering and handling and would be better mounted to the motorcycle frame. I have found if mounted properly the windscreen can do its job without a negative effect on handling, the key being not to mount a front piece so big that wind can easily push the motorcycle around by putting uneven pressure on the handlebars through the windscreen.

Once the windscreen is in place, then mount the gas tank panniers. These come from various sources, but I prefer models offered by Acrostich/Riderwearhouse. These drape over the gas tank and attach to

A father-son team from Anchorage, Alaska, start up the road to Deadhorse. In the first 100 miles they rode through a forest fire, then rain 200 miles farther north, and snow on the Atigun Pass before reaching Deadhorse, all in the same day.

ELECTRIC RIDING GEAR

Electric cold-weather riding gear has made staying warm easier. If you go for the full package you can add electric gloves, socks, jacket, and pants liners. By the time you are done you have wires and connectors running everywhere, but you will be warm and toasty.

The electric riding gear started with electric vests and the premise that if the upper body, torso, and organs remain warm the body will continue to push warm blood to the toes and fingers. The earlier heated vests gave rise to entire systems. There is no argument that once you are wired from neck to toe and your system is operating properly you will be warm.

One downside to the electric clothing is it is bulky. That is because it is constructed with two layers that electric warming wires run in between. If you put on your electric socks and try to get your riding boot on you will find it's a struggle, often requiring a second pair of oversize boots. I have also found the electric gloves to be more bulky than I like for flexibility of my hands. I prefer heated grips on my handlebars to the heated gloves.

As for the electric pants liners, they are not easily slipped into on the side of the road, requiring the removal of my outer pants and a place to comfortably do the job.

I have gone from the electric vest to a full electric jacket liner because it can also be used as a jacket by itself for the night or as cool weather walking-around wear, as well as my pillow when I want to roll it up.

Another factor to consider before purchasing a full set of electric riding gear is where are you going to store it on your touring motorcycle when it is not needed? A full set easily takes up one saddlebag or aluminum pannier, and that is a lot of space to give up. The gear is ideal for a day ride when it is cold. You can suit-up and plug-in before leaving your garage, then ride for the day percolating away. But sooner or later you will want to put your regular gloves, boots, and possibly jacket back on, leaving you with a storage problem if on the road for an extended tour. My personal space, weight, and budget formula has a full electric liner on my touring bike. When the cold sets in I stop, put on and plug in my electric liner, then pull my rain boots on over my riding boots to cut the wind and keep some warmth in. I do the same with my gloves and pants. If I have heated handgrips on the motorcycle I switch them on, and the same with the seat warmer.

Another downside to the electric riding gear is it takes electricity. I have read a couple of pieces about how much the electric wear draws and how that falls within the output system of various motorcycles. While that is true, and most big bikes have enough juice to pump some excess to the liner wires, some motorcycle models only put out those figures at certain rpm and above. My BMW GS motorcycle, even when brand new, did not have enough juice at lower rpm to keep its own system charged. While tooling on the interstate at 5,000 to 6,000 rpm it was able to keep the battery charged, but when I was running around town at rpms below 4,000 the system bled heavily. I was one unhappy and sweaty motorcyclist when I had to push start my heavily laden BMW on a flat street while wearing my electric riding gear and dragging its connecting wires on the ground with cars and trucks honking at me. Poking around town while plugged-in and turned-on had drained the lifeblood out of my bike's battery to the point where the starter would not work.

the motorcycle main frame with bungee cords. These soft-sided bags, slightly larger than a shoebox, are perfect for carrying items like a quart of oil, spare inner tubes, gloves, and raingear. Mounted properly, my knees tuck in behind them. As rain is pushed down from the windscreen, instead of hitting my knees and lower legs it hits the hanging tank panniers and is further directed downward or outward, away from my lower body.

For the water that slips by the lower part of the windscreen and is blown backwards and upwards, I have a waterproof tank bag mounted on the gas tank that it hits. Wind pushes the wet around the tank bag and, if I am moving fast enough, around my upper torso that is pressed to the back of it.

Something to take care with is the mounting of the pannier or tank bag system to ensure they are far enough back not to interfere with the steering or make hard contact with the windscreen. An oversized tank bag can make the steering unmanageable at slow speeds, like when trying to make a slow speed turn or doing off-road maneuvering.

Another word of caution about windscreens is to make sure they are high enough to deflect wind over your head at speed to avoid buffeting, which can be as tiring as fighting the wind itself. Not only does the buffeting become an annoyance and stressful, tiring you, but the wind noise itself can also tire you. To avoid tiring from

Ready for the far north where it can be snowing on a forest fire in July, I caught this rider as he headed toward the Arctic Circle. He said he had ridden three days in the rain before I met him and had stayed dry in his riding suit.

wind noise, wear earplugs where they are legally allowed.

To deflect the water off your hands, mount hand protectors on the end of the handlebars. These are sold as protectors for the levers in case of a crash, but a larger pair properly mounted can also serve as deflectors of water, diverting the water up, down, and sideways, away from the hands.

With the above "budget system" I can save nearly $1,000 over the price of mounting a full fairing to the front of my motorcycle and gain storage space and ease of access for things stored in the panniers or tank bag.

The second line of defense from the water is a wet-weather riding suit. These are lined or unlined shells made of some material that is rubberized or coated with polyvinyl chloride (PVC). They have on their plus side that they are waterproof and cut the wind. They have on their minus side that they seal your body so well that they trap water and moisture inside, as from perspiration.

Rain suits come in either one- or two-piece designs with various methods for closing or sealing the unit. I prefer the two-piece models for three reasons. First, getting into a one-piece rain suit is a struggle. While I can slip my booted feet into the pants with

Another word of caution about windscreens is to make sure they are high enough to deflect wind over your head at speed to avoid buffeting, which can be as tiring as fighting the wind itself.

An American rider on a German touring machine presents a brightly colored image for other drivers to see, an additional plus to his being dry and warm. Padded shoulders, hips, elbows, and knees, plus a back protector, add to the rider's protection.

Waxed cotton was the English answer to wet weather riding in the last century. It has since lost ground to plastic, nylon, rubber, and Gore-Tex. If you wear waxed cotton you soon learn to take it off before sitting on anything that shows dirt because the wax collects dirt and leaves it on white chairs, light-colored davenports, or fabric car seats.

As the British riders moved into the twenty-first century they adopted more protective and water-resistant riding clothing. A spray can of water repellent is usually all that is needed to refresh the resistance factor on textile riding gear, and these silicone sprays do not collect dirt like the wax formerly used on cottons.

ease, I always struggle getting the upper half over my shoulders to get it on, then again to get it off.

The second reason is I can wear one piece of the two-piece suit, as I often do the jacket, when I'm not riding but walking around town or the campground in the rain.

The third is it is easier to store the two pieces separately, like in the pockets of my fairing, than the one large one-piece unit, which wads up bigger.

There are several options to keep your feet and hands dry. I wear waterproof riding boots to solve the wet foot problem, although I do carry waterproof boot covers for when the wet becomes serious. To keep my mitts dry I like the three-fingered gloves offered by Aerostich. They fold up small,

are 100 percent waterproof, and their three-finger design does not restrict my hand movement on the controls like some of the rubberized all-finger gloves do.

"I can ride through it." At my age I should know that believing I am going to be able to ride through a rain storm or cloud burst and stay dry is about as likely as an elephant doing a back flip. I know it is a hassle to stop and suit up when I see the dark and wet ahead, but the number of times I have ended up soaked and cold should have taught me the hassle is worth it. What fools me is the passage of time and how that cold and wet feeling dims as the experience falls into the distance. I should have printed on the inside on my face shield, "I am not going to ride through it and I am going to be wet and cold, very wet and cold, and miserable like the last time." Or maybe it should simply read, "Elephants cannot do back flips."

In an emergency, a rain suit can be made out of plastic garbage bags. Punch arm and head holes in one and put it on your upper body, then leg holes in another and step into it, bring it up to your armpits. Use two for your legs and feet and one for each arm. Duct tape everything to prevent the bags from billowing and blowing apart. The system is not pretty, but for the price of a box of garbage bags and some duct tape at the local supermarket, you are dry for a while, maybe long enough to ride through the storm.

What appears to be a perfect riding day in Wyoming can quickly turn into a torrential downpour. This rider was prepared for what he saw approaching from the west. Those clouds mean rain, and he found himself riding in a heavy cloud burst an hour later. His riding clothing kept him dry and warm until the summer storm passed.

Three-fingered "Spock" rain gloves from Aerostich now are a standard in my touring kit. They fold up to about the size of a wadded handkerchief. They're 100 percent waterproof, they quickly and easily slip over my riding gloves, and they leave lever/throttle management unencumbered.

One world tourer's solution for staying dry was to ride in the truck he had following him. When he saw a rain cloud approaching, or woke up in the morning to drizzle, he would have his helpers load the motorcycle into the chase truck and ride out the storm in the cab. With this system he was able to wear his leather riding jacket and pants on his ride around the world and not worry about the expense or appearance of Gore-Tex, electric suits, or rain gear. Chances are good you won't have this luxury available to you.

KEEPING COOL

On the other side of staying warm and dry is staying cool. Whether riding across the Sahara Desert or from Barstow to Las Vegas in July, heat can hurt you just as much as cold and wet.

Leather is hot in warm weather and loses its protective value when you take it off or unzip it. The all-weather riding suit that keeps you warm in the cold weather and reasonably dry in the wet can cook you in the heat. Although the material is porous and allows moisture out, it is still hot, espe-

cially when stopped and idling around town in congested traffic sitting over your hot running engine.

My solution for hot-weather riding gear is the nylon mesh jackets and pants offered

Wet-weather touring gear from Russia. I met these riders in the middle of Siberia. They were making a two-week tour to a Russian motorcycle rally. The rain suits were made for fishermen to wear on ocean fishing boats. While waterproof, they were bulky and melted when they came close to exhaust pipes or engine cooling fins.

This English couple had come "overland" to Thailand. Their touring suits were worn no matter how hot the weather was. They claimed the suits breathed enough when they were moving to keep them from expiring from heat, plus they did not want to ride in high accident countries without adequate body protection.

Some riders won't let go of their leather riding gear. Here the "GT Rider" from Thailand is shown still wearing a leather jacket and high leather boots. I photographed him in Laos on a day when it was nearly 90 degrees. While he said he didn't notice the heat after living in that area for years, I was sweating profusely and I was riding in a nylon mesh shirt.

in various forms by several companies. These are padded with various protective materials to allow for protection from a possible crash. They are also lightweight, stuff into smaller spaces than my regular riding gear, and allow the wind to cool my body while riding.

When I tour with my nylon mesh riding gear I use my rain suit as my cool weather gear, wearing it over my mesh. My boots are the same waterproof boots I always wear; however, I do move to a lighter-weight glove.

For hot weather riding I prefer short gloves that are perforated to allow for good airflow and that have a padded leather palm. The padding is for two reasons, the first is to absorb some of the engine and road vibrations that reach my wrists and arms through the ends of the handlebars. The second is for protection when I fall.

I said "when," not "if." Any dedicated motorcyclist with any miles under his or her belt will tell you that you are going to fall sooner or later, it is just a matter of time.

My solution for hot-weather riding gear is the nylon mesh jackets and pants offered in various forms by several companies.

Whether at slow speed or fast, when that happens I want something between my skin and the pavement or gravel. When I see a rider wearing fingerless gloves when it is hot, I know they are betting foolishly. If they could so easily predict when their crash is going to happen, it would be on that day they would stay home and watch TV. I have torn up some pretty expensive lightweight riding gloves, thankful each time to have

For the hot climates, like here in Laos at the Plain of Jars, I use a nylon mesh riding shirt from Bohn Body Armor and nylon mesh pants. I want the padded body protection body armor gives while being lightweight and breathing. I look at this touring gear as an investment in my safety and well being.

had something between my palms and fingers and the pavement.

One of the considerations with mesh or lightweight gloves is to cover any exposed skin with sunblock. It only takes a few hours for the tops of my exposed hands to burn, so I usually smear the gooey stuff on at the start of the day when using my lightweight gloves.

To cool my head I use a vented flip-up helmet. When riding at speed I open the vents that allow air to pass through the helmet, some by the vacuum created by air blowing by, and some from air being pushed through as it hits the top of my helmet.

If I am wearing a riding suit made of textile and it has large pockets, I fill them with ice from a motel vending machine or fast-food restaurant before riding off into the heat. The ice melts, and eventually the suit dries, but I am given a slight reprieve from the heat.

When driving at slow speed I can flip up the front of the helmet to let my face and head breathe even more, although I know this is not wise. One of my BMW riding friends was doing the same thing with his BMW flip-up helmet when he had one of his slow speed tip-overs. He lost both front teeth.

There are large blood vessels passing through your neck to the heart, and a large artery going the other direction. Cooling down the blood as it flows past helps your whole body feel like it is cooler. An inexpensive way to do that is to wet a handkerchief and tie it around your neck. An even better way, for a few dollars more, is a Kool-Off Tie sold by Aerostich/Riderwearhouse. These are cloth wraps with moisture-retaining granules on the inside. Soak them in water overnight and they will empty a large glass of water, then wear it around your neck for the day and they will cool you

HELMETS: ESSENTIAL PROTECTION

A helmet is something I wear whether it is hot or cold, even just riding one block to my neighborhood 7-Eleven. There's something about that satisfying bug splat on my face shield at 70 miles per hour that makes me appreciate having my helmet. Or the rain hitting the face shield, or a rock thrown up by a passing car or truck. Once I had a bird fly into my helmet, wedging itself between my uplifted face shield and the helmet, a lucky event for me that it did not go into the opening, and an unlucky event for the bird.

A female tourer once told me that if I rode a Harley-Davidson I would not need to wear a helmet. Several years later I am still trying to figure out how she arrived at that conclusion. Other arguments I have yet to be sold on include how helmets restrict my vision (only if my eyes are on the sides or in the back of my head), how they restrict my ability to hear things (to cut down on wind fatigue that is exactly what I want to happen), and how their weight contributes to a broken neck in a crash (I would rather have a broken neck than half a face or brain).

One of the things I have learned is to hydrate myself while riding. The direct sun on my body and the wind passing by both dehydrate me as the water being sweated out of me evaporates, especially in the dry heat of the deserts.

off. If you want an even cooler wrap, after they have soaked up the water in the glass, toss them in the refrigerator for a few hours. They stay surprisingly cool for many miles.

When it is really hot I will take my mesh riding jersey or T-shirt off and soak them in water, then pour some on my pants, soaking through to my underwear. While the first shock of cool water can straighten your hair, when it is over and I am riding there is a pleasantly cool feeling as the wind blows by. After an hour or so I am ready to get my hair straightened again.

I have managed the desert heats of Australia, Africa, and South America, the sweltering jungles of Asia, and our own Arizona and Nevada when temperatures were hot enough to fry eggs on the hood of a car. One of the things I have learned is to hydrate myself while riding. The direct sun on my body and the wind passing by both dehydrate me as the water being sweated out of me evaporates, especially in the dry heat of the deserts. By the time I realize I am thirsty I have reached a dangerous point. My answer is to start the day with a reserve by tanking up before riding, then refilling my body every time I stop. I do this with either water or some energy drink that is designed to replace the electrolytes I am losing. If I am riding without stopping, I drink water from bottles I keep in my tank bag, which I can easily do with the front of my flip-up helmet in the up position.

That's China behind me. It was April and approaching the "hot" season in North Vietnam. I started the morning in a cold rain wearing everything I had with a light nylon raincoat over my riding gear. By noon it was sweltering and I was down to my lightweight touring clothes.

An alternative to my mesh riding gear is what this rider chose for a top, a Knox Body Guard shirt. With padded elbows and shoulders and a built-in back protector, it gives body protection while feeling as if you are riding without a shirt. Her big surprise was the day she left the front unzipped and a bee went down the opening.

The keys to staying warm, dry, and cool depend on how much you are willing to invest in your personal well-being, safety, and comfort.

A fool's proverb is one that says it is wise to stop and have a "cool one" while riding to cool down. Sure, the air-conditioning in the bar provides some short-term relief, but the alcohol in the beer(s) you suck down can kill you. Not only is alcohol a diuretic that can cause you to lose more liquid than you put in, but the effects of it can give you that "buzz" that can kill you while riding.

The keys to staying warm, dry, and cool depend on how much you are willing to invest in your personal well-being, safety, and comfort. I look at specialized riding gear, like my Bohm body protection shirt and padded mesh pants, as an investment in my safety as well as increasing my personal comfort factors. It was a hard awakening to find I was touring South America with riding gear that cost more than my motorcycle!

ROOM AND BOARD

WHAT YOU WILL LEARN

- **How to find deals on food and lodging**

- **Security tips to keep you, your bike, and your belongings safe**

- **Camping tips and gear recommendations**

Not my favorite eatery, but you know what to expect, except in India where there will be no beef in the burger. For the budget traveler, fast food offers the best value, and is often less expensive than preparing your own. This McDonald's was a treat after eating lots of rice and fish, a common fare as I toured Taiwan.

Whether to eat and sleep indoors or outdoors is an element of motorcycle touring that has an effect on everything from budget to tire wear to the handling of the motorcycle. The added weight of camping gear can add to the length of your tour, but the dollars spent eating in restaurants or sleeping in hotels will greatly increase the cost. Both plans can add to your frustrations if you are not prepared.

EATING

Where, when, and what to eat can set the pace of your tour. If you are a budget tourer, someone who wants to maximize their miles while minimizing expenses, then the full-service restaurants offering multicourse meals are not your fare.

On the other hand if you are a connoisseur of fine foods, wishing to indulge your pallet at the expense of your wallet, then the upscale eateries are where you vector at feeding time.

One of my motorcycle journalist acquaintances rates his tours by the satisfaction of his pallet. If you ask him how his tour of Italy was, he recounts how fine the wine was at a four-star hotel restaurant on

I try to maintain

a balanced diet when

on the road.

Lake Como. When asked about his ride in Argentina he rolls his eyes, pulls on his goatee, and purports the steak he had in Bariloche was the finest in the world. Listening to him pontificate about the food consumed during his tour you would think he was on a restaurant tour and not a motorcycle tour because he rarely mentions what roads were the best or where the scenery was superb. For him, the eating and shared tales around the table after a day of riding

One of the most expensive countries in the world to tour by motorcycle, if not *the* most expensive, is Japan. I learned to cut my meals down to twice a day. A breakfast at Denny's still set me back twice what it would have cost in the United States.

are more important than the touring.

I fall somewhere between the budget tourer and the restaurant rider when it comes to eating. While I try to maintain a balanced diet when on the road, I know that eating in restaurants is generally going to cost me more than cooking my own food. I also know that most restaurant food is fried and not baked, a type of preparation that my waist size does not need.

If I am traveling alone I usually start my day with a light morning snack and possibly coffee or tea, then another light meal at noon. After I have reached my destination for the day I park the motorcycle and enjoy a large evening meal. Often my midday meal is little more than a few items picked up at the local market or supermarket and thrown in the tank bag. I snack while riding. This way I am able to cut down on lost time waiting for my food to be prepared in a restaurant and I avoid the higher costs.

I once traveled with a friend who had to have what he called "three square meals" each day. I noted that each morning it took us an extra hour to get on the road while he enjoyed his breakfast. At noon we would stop again and another hour was spent while taking in a large lunch. I enjoyed these times because we could talk about the roads we had been riding, our personal and business affairs, and other shared interests. However, I had to adjust my daily riding expectations

by nearly 100 miles to allow for the lost time. I also had to adjust my budget upwards to accommodate the nearly 100 percent increase in my food and drink costs.

SLEEPING

To sleep in a hotel, motel, guesthouse, or hostel depends on your lifestyle and budget much the same as your eating choices. The comfort and amenities of a four-star hotel are priorities for some tourers. They feel the most secure sleeping in a hotel that has a foil-covered chocolate on the pillow and turn-down service while their motorcycle is safe and secure in the locked garage below.

I snack while riding. This way I am able to cut down on lost time waiting for my food to be prepared in a restaurant and I avoid the higher costs.

ALCOHOL

I never consume alcohol at meals if I have to ride anywhere afterwards. Stupidly, I used to think I could have a beer with lunch, then continue with my riding day until dinner. Sometimes I would ride to dinner, have a beer or two with a large meal, and then ride back to my hotel or motel. The death of friends, increased knowledge about how alcohol can affect driving abilities, skyrocketing insurance rates, and increased enforcement of stiffer alcohol- and drug-related laws have all led me to a hard and fast rule: I do not drink and drive. At the end of the day I park the bike, cover it, and then have my swill. I am so firm in this rule it even spills over to whom I choose to ride with. If my touring partners insist on consuming alcohol and riding, I ride on alone. To take that a step further, I do not ride with anyone, anywhere, anytime who is a drug user.

I'll be the first to suggest sleeping indoors when feeling sick or needing to quickly get warm and dry. The downside to motels is they are expensive ($100 and up per night in some places, like Daytona during BikeWeek, or Alaska), and I seldom get a chance to meet people like I do in a public campground.

THEFT AND SECURITY

One disadvantage to the larger chain motels is the motorcycle may have to be parked several floors below the sleeper, well out of his or her sights. This makes it a target for thieves. To avoid the possible loss of smaller items like tank panniers, bungee cords, and other accessories, the owner should take them off the motorcycle and keep them in the room.

However, the $150 to $300 a night cost is often outside the reach of many travelers.

A chain motel provides a more reasonable expense for a night's sleep; however, these also can be quite expensive, especially during high season, like Bike Week in Sturgis. A $45 room in a seedy motel often commands $150 or more during these peak periods.

While touring through Russia, I saved several thousands of dollars by opting to take my chances with roadside motels versus letting a tourist agency book me into the Russian government tourist hotels. To get a visa to travel through Russia I used an authorized Russian tourist agency. They

Almost nothing will stop the determined thief wanting to take your motorcycle from outside your hotel or motel room

A guesthouse in Germany provided a 50 percent savings over staying in a hotel. These are often owned and operated by a family who live in the same building. The lower level will often have a restaurant and bar for meals and swill. I much prefer these over hotels because they are more friendly, and I often make friends in the evening who appreciate a two-wheel traveler wanting to eat where many of the locals eat.

were able to "stand good" for me while I was in Russia because I needed a business or organization to do so to secure the visa. They required that I purchase a minimum of three nights lodging in one of their approved Russian hotels. These were all expensive and located in inner cities, several approaching luxurious. When I took only the three nights, at between $75 and $100 each, they expressed their surprise saying they had just booked another motorcyclist from the United States for every night of his ride across Russia. While I was sleeping in $5 and $10 rooms, he had opted for the more expensive tour package.

My guess is that he paid as much for sleeping as I paid for my gas, food, drink, and fun combined on my ride across Russia. While none of the rooms I slept in were four-star, all were dry and clean and the people I met were overly friendly. On the other hand, the people I met in the tourist hotels were generally business-like and cold, leaving me with little in the way of a warm feeling for the town or hotel.

For security purposes, I not only depend on my fork lock but also either a chain through the wheels or another type of wheel lock. It is much harder to cut or break these than it is to snap a fork lock by force.

Almost nothing will stop the determined thief wanting to take your motorcycle from outside your hotel or motel room, but one night in Bogota, Colombia, my wheel cable lock did. I was sleeping three floors above my motorcycle, which was parked, covered, and locked off the sidewalk and near the front door of the hotel. Near dawn, one of the front desk employees came to my room to tell me that my motorcycle was laying in the street. Two or more thieves had lifted the locked front wheel up and tried to roll the motorcycle away on the back wheel. After two turns of the back wheel the cable through the rear wheel became so bound up they could roll it no farther, nor were there enough of them to carry the motorcycle off. They threw it down in the street and ran away. With the help of the hotel employee I was able to get it righted and on the center stand, then unwind the rear wheel. While

The mom-and-pop motels are often an inexpensive alternative to the upscale hotels and motels in the city or along the interstates. I like these not only because they are inexpensive, but because I can usually park my motorcycle next to my sleeping space to give me a sense of security.

PANNIERS

Definition: Storage boxes, usually made of metal, plastic, or fiberglass, that secure to the rear fender. Usually larger than stock saddlebags, they are uniquely suited to carry large amounts of gear and equipment, ideal for touring.

A side note on wheel locks and chains: It is very embarrassing and dangerous to ride off forgetting they are still in place.

A mom-and-pop motel can be a more secure option to the larger chain motels. While these are generally clean and less expensive than the chain motels, they sometimes lack traveler amenities like high-speed Internet connections, 100-channel cable TV with remote control, and in-room coffeemakers. What they usually do offer is a parking space for the motorcycle directly in front of the room. While no substitute for guarded indoor parking, carrying the items you remove from the motorcycle at night will take less work and the fact that you are sleeping only feet away may deter unwanted visitors.

One journalist wrote that he tied a string between his big toe and the motorcycle at night, which I'm sure was more bravado than fact. I can picture people tripping over his string all night as they walked by, but it made for a good laugh while reading it. The fact that the motorcycle is near your room does not mean it is any safer. Stories abound of motorcycles being stolen while parked in any situation. Common sense tells you that if the thief wanted your motorcycle and did not want to pull on your big toe all they would have to do is cut your string. On the other hand, it is not so

Worried about your motorcycle being taken at night? Touring through Zimbabwe, Africa, I stayed in a motel one night that provided these two guards to sit by my parked motorcycle for the night. A gunshot awoke me around midnight. One of the guards had shot a suspected thief who had climbed over the walls of the enclosed compound. They dispatched him at point blank range, saying it "sends a message to others."

the thieves had been smart enough to know about the fork lock, they had not counted on the rear wheel chain.

A Russian truck stop motel gave me an inexpensive place to sleep with the security of locking my motorcycle in an enclosed truck parking lot. While the room did not have a private in-room toilet or bath, it did have clean sheets and a soft bed. For $5 I was warm, dry, and happy after a long, cold, wet day of riding.

easy to disarm a noisy alarm or other locking system that has been installed on your motorcycle for such occasions.

I carry a motorcycle cover and use it each night to cover my motorcycle, no matter where I park it. Whether in a gated and guarded garage or parked in front of my room, I have learned that I have fewer uninvited visitors and their fingers on my motorcycle when it is completely covered.

The motorcycle cover has several other uses, such as when I want to leave the motorcycle parked while I explore and take photographs, like in the parking lot at Mount Rushmore. I throw the cover over the motorcycle and secure it, knowing at least the casual passerby cannot see what they might want to touch or steal, like my tank bag or sunglasses. A determined thief, however, will scoff at the bike cover. In a public square in Morocco, with hundreds of people around, the thieves not only took items from my tank bag such as my tire pressure gauge and tourist book, they took the bike cover too!

Another use for the bike cover is as a ground cloth while working on the motorcycle in a parking lot or on dirt. It can also be used to cover the ground or an unhealthy looking picnic table when taking a nap.

In a heavy rain I once pulled over, parked, and covered not only the motorcycle but also myself while we waited for the rain to stop. I was drier than I would have been had I struggled into my rain suit and stood around in the rain.

One item that I carry in my touring kit for sleeping is a lightweight, extra large-travel sheet. This is like a large sack, but it wads up into a shoe-sized stuff sack and is available from better camping stores. It serves as a liner for sleeping bags or as a sack for protection when sleeping in motels with sheets of questionable cleanliness. Sometimes I use it as my only sleeping cover, especially in hot and humid climates. Mine is large enough that it easily goes over my shoulders, leaving only my head exposed to insects. With a little Deet insect

To find the mom-and-pop motels, you often have to get away from the main roads and travel through a town.

A step down from a motel is renting a cabin. For $50 less per night than a motel, this Alaskan cabin had a wood burning heater but no television, telephone, or bathroom. What it did have was a great view of a quiet lake where wild ducks quacked until dark, and then the frogs took over.

There are numerous lodging alternatives. These include guesthouses and pensions in Europe, bed and breakfasts, farm stays, hostels, and backpacker hotels.

Restaurants can pull money out of your wallet faster than gas stations or tollbooths on toll roads. I could not help myself from stopping at this restaurant in Thailand that featured motorcycles on display and around the tables. One was even on a lift. Called "Garage," the owner designed it around a motorcycle repair shop. The food was reasonably priced and the appointments perfect for a gearhead traveler.

repellant on my exposed portions, I am able to avoid mosquito and spider bites. The travel sheet can also serve as an alternate to carrying a bulky sleeping bag if you throw your riding suit over the top to keep the warmth in and cold out, and your rain suit underneath as ground cover. It is a new addition to my touring kit, but now I seldom travel without it.

To find the mom-and-pop motels, you often have to get away from the main roads and travel through a town. Along Interstate 40, crossing Oklahoma, New Mexico, and Arizona, you often find the

newer chain motels near the major interchanges. But if you drive a little farther off the interstate and into the towns, you come to what was formerly the main street, often being the original Route 66. Along these former main thoroughfares are numerous small motels that were once the main tourist rest points for the night. Staying here can give the traveler a real taste of the Mother Road across America, something not found in the chain motels near the interstate.

If you are approaching a major town or city and looking for a reasonable motel, try to pass through the major portion of the urban area before settling on one for the night. In the morning you will miss the rush hour commute into the city and be away from the city much quicker with less stress. It is a fresher way to start your day.

To save money I often stop at public markets and purchase my lunch for a picnic later in the day. I can cut my midday meal expenses in half and often enjoy the fresh air more than I would the midday rush at a restaurant.

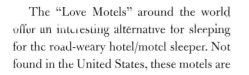

Between a cabin and a tent was this stucco teepee. I usually carry a small sleeping bag and inflatable mattress when I am touring for places like this. I don't use them every night, but there are times when I decide to use a cabin or something close to it where they are preferable to sleeping under some well-used blankets on a lumpy mattress.

The "Love Motels" around the world offer an interesting alternative for sleeping for the road-weary hotel/motel sleeper. Not found in the United States, these motels are not for sleeping. They are where couples go to spend a few hours together. I have found them while touring much of Central and South America, Cuba, Japan, and some

INTERACTING WITH LOCALS

When I am traveling outside the United States and locals approach me I have learned it is best to avoid the following:

• Discussing U.S. politics. I usually tell them I do not know much about politics and try to avoid discussing politicians or elections.

• Showing anyone any amount of money. I never disclose where my valuables are stashed.

• Going off to party with the locals, especially when alcohol or drugs are involved. While you may think it is an affront to their friendliness to turn down their invitation, it is unwise to leave your motorcycle and belongings alone. It is unwise to go with your new friends to places you are not familiar with or where you will be unsafe and outnumbered.

A motorcycle tourer in Brazil chose to spend the evening drinking and partying with the locals. In the end they beat him up for no apparent reason. He was lucky to get away with his life.

If I am invited to join a table in a restaurant or bar for a drink, or if the locals want to buy me one, I try to limit my fun to one or two drinks. If I feel the party is getting too rowdy or the locals are getting too friendly, I try to politely excuse myself and return to my room or tent, to the possible dismay of my patrons.

Camping in the wild is the cheapest sleeping while touring. One of the secrets to this form of sleeping is to find a secluded place well away from prying eyes, especially of those who would like to give you a ticket or have you arrested for trespassing. Today this form of camping has almost become an art form as urban sprawl and demands for national security have spread.

One of the downsides to motorcycle touring and camping is the added weight of camping equipment and loss of space.

A Russian "roadhouse." With a restaurant and bar on the lower level, this was a nice $10 sleeping place for the night. Unfortunately, it was full by the time I found it. A Swiss couple and I were allowed to pitch our tents alongside the roadhouse and use the indoor facilities for $2. We spent a memorable evening in the restaurant meeting local people and tourists who dropped in for a drink. We also learned how to swill vodka and yell Russian folksongs, and then did not have to climb stairs when we were done.

places in Southeast Asia. The rooms are usually rented for short periods of time, ranging from two to four hours. As you enter these motel compounds there are numerous stalls or garages where, if open, you drive in and pull a curtain or door closed behind you so no one passing by can see your vehicle (and license number). Often there will be a small two-way mailbox-sized opening in the room or back of the garage where you place your money for the time you want to use the room. At the end of your stay, a bell or knock will be heard meaning your time is up and if you wish to stay longer you must pay more.

Some motels have a checkout office as you leave where you pay for time used before you can exit. Usually you never see or make eye contact with the person taking the money and the transactions are all quite discreet.

The rooms are usually well appointed, with some offering spas, color cable TV with XXX-rated channels, waterbeds, stocked refrigerators, and condom machines. They are always quite clean and an ideal way to freshen up after some days of living hard on the road. All come with seemingly unending hot water, clean sheets, and substantial locking doors.

This was free public camping at the edge of the Wrangell–St. Elias National Park Preserve near McCarthy, Alaska. For a less spectacular view of the Wrangell Mountains I could have paid $150 for a night in the nearby lodge. However, I was warned that bears liked to wander the campground at night, something I would not have worried about in the $150 bedroom.

While trying to find an inexpensive place to spend the night around Tokyo, a Love Motel was the best alternative. Whereas the hotels in the area were $150 and up for a night, eight hours in a Love Motel was half that if I checked in after 11 p.m. and got the "all-night rate."

The one stumbling block when paying for long-term use of a room in a Love Motel is communicating that you want the room for the night and not just a couple of hours. Once over that hurdle you are free to luxuriate in what the owners have to offer. Some are so lavish you may think you have entered a small Disneyland as you ride into the compound.

In between motels and camping are cabins. Most offer electricity, but you seldom find running water and the toilets and bathrooms are usually a walk away. Some come with freshly washed sheets and blankets while others offer only a bed with a mattress.

Cabins usually afford you the opportunity to park your motorcycle nearby. They are also a quaint change from sterile hotel rooms. However, they are sometimes as expensive as a motel room.

Big-displacement motorcycle owners often scoff at the 650-cc touring bike I ride, but I can carry as much gear as they can, maybe more. Here, camping in the wild of Alaska, my bike is carrying everything I need to live on the road, including a large tent, sleeping bag, and mattress. It is not how big your touring bike is, but how well you pack it.

This touring camper had carried the smallest tent I have seen, not much larger than a mummy sleeping bag. I prefer a larger tent and will give up carrying capacity for it. I want one large enough for me to haul all my riding gear into and out of the rain, leaving enough room for me to move around. I also like a higher domed tent so I can get in and out of my clothes vertically.

A rule of thumb I was taught by motorcycle touring friends in Switzerland was "one night sleeping indoors equals four nights on the ground."

If you are planning to stay in cabins you should come prepared with your own sleeping gear, such as a sleeping bag and pillow. In some cabins I find my inflatable camping mattress makes the night more comfortable.

My Kanetsu electric jacket liner from Aerostich is one handy multi-use part of my touring kit that I can turn into a pillow for nights when the proffered head rest leaves much to be desired. This jacket liner not only warms me while riding and serves as a jacket, but it folds up into its own pocket and makes a nice pillow. Even if not folding it up, I often throw it over my cabin or motel pillow with the fleece side out to protect my head from what might be crawling around on the house pillowcase.

There are numerous other alternatives to hotel/motel and cabin camping, depending on where you are touring. These include guesthouses and pensions in Europe, bed and breakfasts, farm stays (New Zealand), hostels, rinkons (Japan), hospedajes and casas familial (Central and South America), and backpacker hotels.

CAMPING

While touring New Zealand and Australia, as well as parts of Europe, I can often slept dry and cheaply in trailers that were available in campgrounds. These were less expensive than a motel, and never had a toilet, but they often had working stoves, televisions, and all had electricity. These trailers were a nice way to get out of the motels and into the campgrounds without having to bother with carrying camping equipment other than a sleeping sack or light sleeping bag. It was in the campgrounds that I met the most people while I traveled, as many felt comfortable in approaching me while I was doing maintenance on the motorcycle. They often had great curiosity about a motorcycle traveler and were always surprised to find that I was an American because they seldom, if ever, met Americans traveling alone.

Camping while touring is as large a subject as motorcycle touring itself, with many books and organizations dedicated to the topic. For the beginner, a good primer book is *Motorcycle Camping Made Easy* by Bob Woofer. For the more advanced camper, there is *Camping's Top Secrets* by Cliff Jacobson, though it is not specific to motorcyclists. If you are in a joining mood, consider signing up as a member of the International Brotherhood of Motorcycle Campers (P.O. Box 375, Helper, UT 84526, www.inmc.org).

The cheapest, and often most rewarding, camping associated with motorcycle touring is the unauthorized camping, camping where there are no attendants to collect your money, no motorhomes with generators running all night, and no kids noisily splashing around the communal swimming pool.

One of the downsides to motorcycle touring and camping is the added weight of camping equipment and loss of space. While two riders on one motorcycle can manage camping their way around the world, and some have, I think that form of touring is best limited to short tours, like a long weekend. There is considerably more freedom and a lot less weight when each rider goes solo with his or her own gear.

One way to save money while touring and camping is to share a camping spot with another motorcyclist. Four of us were usually able to share a campsite when we were camping in RV parks and private campgrounds on our ride to Alaska. While the RVs were paying $50 for the night, my riding pals and myself were each paying $12.50 with our tents and motorcycles on one site.

The price of a campsite can sometimes meet or exceed the price of a motel room at a mom-and-pop motel, making camping less attractive than sleeping indoors. On the other hand, during peak times and high tourism seasons, the price for pitching a tent versus sleeping inside may be as much as 400 percent less.

A rule of thumb I was taught by motorcycle touring friends in Switzerland was "one night sleeping indoors equals four nights on the ground." The savings by camping versus hotels can easily pay for the price of a tent and sleeping bag in a short few days on the road.

Your tent and sleeping bag do not have to be the most expensive either. I have often used a $45 tent and $50 sleeping bag for a couple of weeks, then tossed them away as used. The money I saved sleeping outdoors paid for the tent and bag after a couple of days, and the rest of the savings were used to finance my tour.

I like to check-in to the private campgrounds from time to time. Although more expensive than public camping areas like state or city parks, these offer many more

amenities. For instance, if I have been on the road for several weeks and need to take a break for laundry and motorcycle maintenance, a private campground is ideal. I can use their washing machines and not have to leave my motorcycle parked outside a busy laundromat in some busy urban setting. I can also do minor maintenance (sometimes major) on my campsite and not have to rent some inside shop space to do things like change oil or check valve clearances. The private campgrounds will also receive mail and packages for me, holding them for my arrival, if I make arrangements in advance. I have had tires and motorcycle parts sent from mail order houses ahead of me to campgrounds, and they were waiting when I arrived.

Once while riding in a part of the Midwest, I could not easily reach the next campground as the rain started to tire me. As dark was setting in I spotted a self-serve car wash. Because it was late and raining it

Touring alone in Africa. There are pluses and minuses to pitching your tent under a tree. Things fall out of trees onto your tent, and lightening likes to hit trees. But here I was trying to stay out of the path of the rhinos that roamed freely in the enclosed rhino park where I was camping.

One of the first things I do when I get a new tent is make sure there are extra tent pegs to replace the ones I will eventually lose or break.

I camped next to this lonely tree in the desert of Tanzania hoping not to have to climb it at night if I had unwelcome visitors that walked on four legs. While the price of camping was cheap (free), I slept very lightly and left at dawn. The next night I paid for an indoor bed and some sleep.

was not being used. I pulled my motorcycle in, covered it in my dark motorcycle cover, and pitched my tent. The one police officer who checked on me asked that I be out early in the morning, which I was. That night of

camping was free and dry.

The one item that has moved from its previous designation as "nice to have, if I have the space" to my "essential" category for camping is an inflatable air mattress. I

With 24 hours of light near the Arctic Circle you can skip the $145 per night hotel and catnap on the side of the road. I caught this tourer doing just that before he started up the Haul Road.

used to use my riding gear and rain suit to sleep on. It was a lumpy mattress but better than the roots and stones under the tent. Then I discovered the compact inflatable mattresses. While they are expensive and take up valuable storage space, they make sleeping on the ground far more comfortable. In the morning I am better rested and my muscles do not feel stiff and sore. An added feature is that the inflatable mattress serves as an insulator, keeping away cold when sleeping on permafrost, like in Siberia or Alaska, and heat from the baked ground of the Australian outback.

One of the first things I do when I get a new tent is make sure there are extra tent pegs to replace the ones I will eventually lose or break. If the ones that come with the tent are flimsy or junk, I throw them away and replace them with something sturdy enough to beat into loose rocks and long enough to provide support in sand.

Another thing I do is cut a plastic ground cloth the exact size of the tent bottom. I put this down on wet grass, or if there is any possibility of rain, to keep moisture from seeping into my tent from the bottom. I also throw it down on rocks or anything else that can puncture the floor of my tent.

When checking into a campground in Australia I was given a hand drill after I paid my nightly fee. When I asked what it was for, the owner told me it was for drilling holes in the sun-baked earth to drive my tent pegs into. The ground was nearly rock hard and radiated heat like an oven all night.

There are many tips and tricks that can make camping more comfortable for the motorcycle tourer. After years of packing useless equipment, cleaning things I don't end up using, and trying to plan for every situation, I have gotten the tasks down to a comfort level where I do not miss the lost space or the added weight. The payoff has been many memorable evenings spent in the quiet solitude of a perfect setting knowing that only me, my motorcycle, and nature were the partners.

This was my pay-off for some hard touring through Africa by motorcycle. My goal had been to tour Zanzibar on two wheels, which I managed after ten years of planning and saving. I could have taken a rental cottage on the beach but decided to roll out the air mattress and sleeping bag on the sands of the Indian Ocean.

STRETCHING YOUR MONEY

Chapter 8

WHAT YOU WILL LEARN

- Ways to save money on lodging and food

- How to deal with currency and exchange rates in foreign countries

- How to construct or improvise inexpensive touring gear

Learn to work on your own motorcycle. At $80 to $100 per hour for labor costs to change your oil, plus $15 per quart for oil and a disposal fee, you can save $150 by doing it on your own. Many auto supply stores let you dispose of the old oil for free.

If you are a high-end New Yorker or film star, someone who cares more about travel and less about the cost, you can skip this chapter. If you are a budget-conscious traveler looking to maximize your time on the road with a fixed amount of money to do it with, there might be some tips here that can help you.

There are some costs of motorcycle touring you can manage and others that are outside your control. Obviously you can manage what you spend for food, whether to spend $50 for dinner or $10. You also have control over deciding to sleep in the Hilton or a hostel dorm room. And you also have control over what you spend on your motorcycle before and during your tour.

HOTELS, MOTELS, AND ALTERNATIVES

One night I was trying to find some cheap sleeping, a place where I could pitch my tent for a few hours on fresh grass that was

quiet. My hunt found me stealthily riding into a local graveyard. You can imagine my surprise when I rode over a tent peg and caught the securing line of another motorcyclist who had the same plan.

There are some costs of motorcycle touring you can manage and others that are outside your control.

We later shared laughs and stories about our secret free camping sites around the world. He said he found the grass in cemeteries is green and soft, often the smell of fresh flowers, usually there is no one around to bother you, and if you get lonely and want to talk there are hundreds of people who have no choice but to listen—your own captive audience.

Stay away from the upscale hotels and motels. Ride past town and away from the major interchanges to find less-expensive lodging for the night. This was a clean and friendly hotel a few miles from Hanoi, but I could have paid three times as much closer to the city. Without the big expenses of advertising and prime location, this small hotel was able to save me 66 percent for an equally nice room.

One of the downsides to cemetery sleeping is you may be unwelcome to do so by local authorities or guardians. It is best to slip in quietly at dusk with your headlight off and be gone early in the morning. I also prefer the graveyards well away from large urban areas as most town cemeteries are often home to some unsavory two-legged animals that hunt for other two-legged prey at night.

Free camping for the night is often near where you might spend $25 to camp in a private or public campground. To find out where, try www.freecampgrounds.com.

Wherever you find free camping, be careful when riding in after dark, you might ride over someone else's tent pegs.

Some travelers lean on club memberships to travel cheaply, calling listed members in their directories for free sleeping for the night as well as free tools and places to work on their motorcycles. These are often the homes of most gracious people looking to provide stranded or broken travelers with an oasis in the desert of expensive travel in times of need.

I know of one foreign traveler who even went so far as to have hosts call or e-mail the

CHEAP SLEEP

Some cheap sleeping sites are listed below:
- **Cheapest Deals**
  (www.cheapestdeals.com)

- **Hostels.com**
  (www.hostels.com)

- **Room Saver**
  (www.roomsaver.com)

- **Camp/campground reservations**
  (www.reserveamerica.com)

- **Savvy Traveler**
  (www.savvytraveler.com)

- **Bed and breakfasts**
  (www.bbonline.com)

This rider dropped $1,800 for a service stop at a dealer while touring across the country. Plan when and what you need done while on the road. Changing your own tires before leaving on a trip can easily save you the price of having to pay full retail and labor costs while on the road.

night, I always try to pay them back with something when I can, whether it be a book I send when I return home, or the offer of reciprocating if they are in my area or have a referred friend in need. I look at these member directories more as an emergency back-up than a way to cut my travel costs, and I am always a paid-up member of the club whose directory I am using.

Rather than dropping your motorcycle off for full maintenance at a local dealer while you are touring, do as much of it yourself as you can, unless the work has to be done professionally to keep your motorcycle covered under the manufacturer's warranty.

If you are going to sleep in a motel or hotel, you might want to shave a few dollars off the price tag by looking away from the larger places toward the smaller ones. I once traveled with a friend who insisted in staying at expensive motels. I complained about the money we were wasting after several nights. He said I was looking at the situation wrong, that he did not mind spending the money because he wanted people to think or know he had money, that he was in an upper income bracket. He argued that he had spent a considerable sum on his motorcycle and riding clothing and wanted people to see that, the kind of people he wanted to attract, and that he would not find them at a motel costing half as much each night. He considered the excess he was paying for his appearances as a form of validation for the excess he had paid for his motorcycling hobby.

next destination for her and broker her stays. Sadly, this traveler had learned to use the system so well she had not even joined the BMW association she was using. She managed to eat and sleep well as she crossed the country, saying her free-loading was not her problem but that of the members who willingly listed their names in the club directory and put her up. The other contributor to her abuse was the person who gave her his club directory and taught her how to use it.

I have used these directories from time to time and always found the listed people very friendly and generous. If I am using their workshop, tools, or spending the

Try buddying-up and splitting the cost of a room. This works well if you can find a

traveling pal you are compatible with sharing a room. This will not work so well in countries where the price for the second person in a room is twice what it is for one person.

Camping is a good alternative to sleeping between clean sheets, but your savings depend on how much you are going to spend on camping equipment. If you are going to spend $500 for a tent, then $250 for a sleeping bag and air mattress, plus the cost for campgrounds each night, you have to do a lot of camping before what you would have spent sleeping indoors equals what you spend for sleeping on the ground.

I also factor into this equation lost riding time, the time I have to spend each morning and evening breaking and making camp. If the purpose of my tour is to ride as much as possible over a short vacation period or long weekend, then I want to get up and be gone each morning and not have to waste riding time packing cumbersome camping equipment, then doing the opposite at the end of the day.

UNEXPECTED COSTS

My touring budgets have often taken unexpected hits, causing my ride to temporarily come to a halt. Once I had to put my plans for a ride through Africa on hold when I realized if I plunged on I was going to be eating sand and pushing my motorcycle for lack of gas somewhere in the middle of the Sahara Desert. The ride through Europe had eaten up four times what I had budgeted. I had not planned on the high cost of gas, food, and some maintenance costs along the way. There was no way I could escape the price of gas, and bad weather had moved me into small hotels and out of campgrounds. The poor

I have never realized any budget savings when shipping a motorcycle by freighter or by sea.

weather had also changed my eating from outside to inside. To try and save some money I had tried to speed up my trip by getting off the small roads and onto the autopistas, which hammered my budget a

Unless your bike is a homemade special like this one, purchase a good service manual for your motorcycle and familiarize yourself with the simple things, like adjusting your chain and checking fluids. While you don't have to be a certified mechanic to adjust your chain, you may deal with some maintenance that requires a computer to diagnose and solve the problem.

For the really budget-conscious there is the option of mixing and matching self-made and manufactured carrying systems. When I saw this box I wanted to ask how many pizzas it would carry, but could not speak the rider's language.

Rather than shipping or flying your motorcycle to other continents, you should consider renting one locally.

RENTING A MOTORCYCLE

With a rental at $10 to $20 per day for a local motorcycle, it makes little economic since to pay $4,000 to fly your own bike for the same two-week tour, not counting the hassles of dealing with local insurance, carnet de passage, handlers to clear your motorcycle through customs, and the same problems upon your return.

bit more because they are expensive toll roads. A cut in a $100 tire found me taking what I could find, which was twice the cost in Switzerland. In Africa, I finally threw in the towel, parked the bike, and returned home to work for some months and sell my truck in order to replenish my travel fund account.

Two British film personalities roared into the BMW shop in Anchorage during their ride around the world on a couple of free bikes from BMW. While their film crew filmed their bikes being worked on, the stars did interviews and hobnobbed with customers. Once the $3,000 of service and repairs were finished, the stars wheelied down the street and waved to the crowd and the bill was sent to BMW. While most of us cannot afford such luxury on a tour (most of us have to buy our own motorcycles and service), there are ways we can get the same done for considerably less.

Rather than dropping your motorcycle off for full maintenance at a local dealer while you are touring, do as much of it yourself as you can, unless the work has to be done professionally to keep your motorcycle covered under the manufacturer's warranty. While I do not like to deal with having to change my own oil, fuel line, and air filters, and then dealing with discarded fluid and cleaning my hands, I have learned to like the $300 to $500 that stays in my wallet.

I have never realized any budget savings when shipping a motorcycle by freighter or by sea. To ship my motorcycle from Denver to South America I was quoted a price of $3,000, which included trucking it from Denver to Long Beach with the freight forwarder providing the crate. To go by air cargo was about $2,000, again by truck, then air cargo. The other major difference was the motorcycle would take 45 days from Long Beach, whereas by air it would be a week.

One traveler I know proudly boasts he never paid for his motorcycle to be shipped as he rode around the world. He would sign on as a worker in the ship's bowels and take his motorcycle aboard as luggage. While he was correct in his claim, I am not sure working for slave wages greasing valves by hand in the hot hold of a ship saves more money than I could make working on my job for the two to three weeks at a real wage rate.

Rather than shipping or flying your motorcycle to other continents, you should consider renting one locally. If you are staying less than a few weeks, then the rental option is budget wise. If rentals are cheap and the customs import process lengthy and cumbersome, then carrying your riding gear on the airplane is the best budget choice. With a rental at $10 to $20 per day for a local motorcycle, it makes little economic since to pay $4,000 to fly your own bike for the same two-week tour, not counting the hassles of dealing with local insurance, *carnet de passage*, handlers to clear your motorcycle through customs, and the same problems upon your return. The $3,000 savings can pay for not only your air fare over and back (say, to Vietnam), but also your two weeks riding around.

EATING CHEAP

One of my touring friends prides himself on how little he spends on food and sleeping while touring. For lunch he has tomato soup, compliments of McDonald's or Burger King. He takes his own cup in, washes and fills it with hot water from the men's room, then adds several spoonfuls of

That $2 bottle of sport drink in the gas station costs half as much at the nearby super-market. The $5 quart of oil can be a fourth of the price at a discount auto parts store.

ketchup from the free dispensers. He finishes with more hot water for a cup of tea using his own tea bags. He often has the audacity to ask for free cream and sugar.

While we often scorn the American fast food places, they usually get high marks amongst the budget tourers for having clean toilets with an unlimited supply of free toilet paper. In many places toilet paper is a premium item, sometimes sold from machines or by attendants. I once went into a public toilet on the French Riviera only to find no paper in the stalls. Then I remembered the woman sitting out front with folded squares of the tissue neatly lined up on a table. I went back out and asked how much, then forked over what I thought to be an outrageous amount. As I swept up the row of paper the old woman started yelling at me. This bandit was charging for one square of the valuable tissue what I thought to be highway robbery for a full row. After that I learned to carry my own very important papers whenever I traveled.

Eating and drinking on the road can whack the healthiest touring budget. My high-end traveling pal who likes to stay in the upscale hotels basks in the luxury of $5 beers in the hotel bar and $40 for the bottle of wine to go along with his $30 dinner in the hotel's restaurant. When I was traveling with him, my beers were coming from the local supermarket at one-fifth the cost, the same with the bottle of wine I would bring back to the room to swill with my take-out meal. What I had saved in a week easily paid for the new battery I needed later.

Try skipping the big and expensive breakfast. Rather than paying the high price for coffee each morning, carry your own instant or quit drinking it altogether. I like to snack out of my tank bag during the day, so I find a market the night before to stock it with small items. While there I buy a container of juice and something small for breakfast.

I also try to cut out my midday meals, especially those heavy lunches where I spend an hour tanking up on greasy fried foods that make me sleepy after I get back on the road. Rather than drop $10 on lunch

Eating and drinking on the road can whack the healthiest touring budget.

If metal or plastic construction costs too much, you can save even more by simply strapping cardboard to your bike like this one in Taiwan.

Think outside the box when designing your touring system. On this BMW the pilot had installed a cheap piece of rope tied to the end of the handlebars so he could sit up straighter and still have control of the bars. While at first glance this "ranch-hand solution" might be laughable, the entrants he beat when he won the 2003 Iron Butt Rally certainly weren't laughing.

and lose an hour of daylight, my lunch out of the tank bag runs a quarter that and I am more alert while riding in the afternoon.

If I do choose to grab a quick lunch on the run I try to stay out of the expensive restaurants where I am paying as much for the appointments and advertising as I am for the food. A quick snack on the side of the road washed down with water or juice cuts on my down time and still gives me a chance to walk around and stretch cramped muscles.

You generally can't get away from the price you have to pay for gasoline unless you know a town well enough to vector into the cheap gas stations. What you spend trying to save a penny or two per gallon is really not going to add up to much unless you are driving a gas guzzler. Where you can save money is by avoiding paying gas station and mini-mart prices for oil and eating. That $2 bottle of sport drink in the gas station costs half as much at the nearby supermarket. The $5 quart of oil can be a fourth of the price at a discount auto parts store. While I was touring Peru I found that a quart of oil in a gas station was four times more expensive than if I went to an oil store, which

were plentiful, and had them fill my used 1-liter plastic container.

CURRENCY AND EXCHANGE

You can also save a few dollars every time you change money by planning ahead. Rather than pay fees for using cash machines to get cash, carry free travelers checks you can get from the American Automobile Association if you are a member. Some banks also offer them free if you have an account with them. In the United States there is no charge for cashing a travelers check; however, to convert them in some foreign countries you can be charged a considerable fee or commission, far more than if you were to convert dollars to the same local currency.

If traveling outside the United States you may save by using local currency to pay your bills over using credit cards. For instance, in Peru and Chile I was often told there would be an additional charge if I used the credit card versus paying with local currency or American dollars. The fee was as much as 8 percent.

If traveling outside the United States you may save by using local currency to pay your bills over using credit cards.

If the exchange rate you are getting from a moneychanger on the street for your American dollars is considerably better than what the banks are offering, it may be time to look that gift horse in the mouth. The moneychangers are most often hustlers, either operating inside or outside government rules.

I was lightly burned once for $20 by a swift-counting street moneychanger.

Knowing I was breaking the law by buying black-market money, I was nervous, as he appeared to be. As he quickly peeled off the bills he looked behind me, whispered loudly, "Police," then handed me the rest of his wad and took off running. I did the same, only to learn what was in the wad was $20 less than I should have gotten.

A second time I was nearly burned for $100. The scam was well done in Peru. I went to a bank to change several $100 bills, the most common dollar denomination. Outside the bank there were several moneychangers offering to give me a rate slightly better than what the bank was offering. Inside the bank there was a long line of customers, so I went back outside to do quick business at a better rate.

On the street outside the bank in Peru I changed four new $100 bills and carefully examined the Peruvian bills I was given in exchange. As I was doing so the money-changer handed me back one of my $100 bills and asked for either part of his change back or another bill because mine had a small tear in the middle where it had been folded. For purposes of making change, most moneychangers and banks want new American dollars, not used ones, and none with any missing corners or tears. Before I leave on a tour I get only new or near new bills from my local bank and I keep these in tightly sealed plastic bags and try not to bend them.

For purposes of making change, most moneychangers and banks want new American dollars, not used ones, and none with any missing corners or tears.

Rather than spend $500 to $1,000 for a larger aftermarket gas tank or fuel cell, try a $10 plastic gas container bungeed on the back like this owner did. If the color bothers you, wrap it in a plastic garbage bag. Throw both away when you are done with them.

Rather than pay $150 for a factory-offered luggage rack, this tourer found what he needed inside a dead refrigerator. He laughed when I asked him about it, saying he could also use it for a cooking grill over the campfire.

I told him the bill could not be mine because all of mine were new and none folded or torn. We had a slight argument, but I finally handed him the $100 back and said, "No, gracias. This bill is counterfeit, let's go to the police." While I was inspecting the change he had given me, he had deftly exchanged his counterfeit bill for one of my good ones. Had I traded him or given him back one fourth the change he had made he would have been able to make a pretty good fee, and I would have been stuck with a worthless bill. It was a good copy, but when I held it up to the sun I saw there was no watermark on the paper, and I knew all of my bills were new, never folded.

USING INEXPENSIVE GEAR

One good way to stretch your money is managing what you spend on your touring motorcycle before you leave on your tour. If you only need your touring equipment for a short time, then consider buying less-expensive equipment.

If you are handy enough or know someone who is, make what you need. A fellow traveler on a similar motorcycle liked my expensive aluminum panniers when he saw them in Guatemala. Rather than pay $1,000 for the expensive European ones to be flown in, he showed mine to a local metal worker who made him a set of copies for $50, including locks. Since the copies were steel and not aluminum, and therefore did not "look" expensive, to get them to match he had them painted with gray aluminum-looking paint. He felt that since he only

Forget the looks and remember your budget when considering spending hundreds of dollars when $10 will work as well.

needed them to get him through South America, why spend $1,000? Better to use that money for sleeping and food, which is what he did.

Rather than spend the $100 to $200 for a back brace so he could sit more upright for those long riding days, one rider used two long belts tied together to go around his back and the fork neck to allow him to lean backwards against something from time to time. It was a $5 system that gave him the same relief the expensive option did.

There is no reason, other than looks, to

Not having the most expensive equipment to make your tour does not mean you are going to fall off the face of the earth without it.

pay for some accessory you will only need for 200 miles on an 8,000-mile trip. Forget the looks and remember your budget when considering spending hundreds of dollars

when $10 will work as well. If you can't stand the way the ugly alternative looks, remember that you can often throw a bag over the top to cover it up, then throw both away when you are done with it, and happily look at what you saved in your wallet.

The options for inexpensive accessories are endless once you focus on saving money over form. Rather than spend several hundred dollars on factory-offered saddlebag liners, one budget-conscious traveler found he could have the same waterproofing and carry-in ability at night with the heavy-duty ski boot plastic bags given away free at the airport during ski season. He always grabbed a couple of extra bags for packing his gear in a $10 Army surplus duffel bag on the back of his motorcycle versus the nearly $200 waterproof water sports bag from the sporting goods store.

One traveling friend insists on wearing bicycle gloves when touring in the hot weather. These leather-palmed gloves are made of nylon and Velcro-closed over his

A simple throttle lock at the motorcycle shop can cost you $30 or more. This rider's out-of-the-box solution was to wrap a wire around the throttle tight enough to hold the throttle open when he pressed it with his thumb down on the brake lever. He said the best wire for this solution comes from the survey flags stuck in the ground alongside roads. It easily bent around the throttle and twisted closed.

If you don't want to spend thousands for a computer, programs, and a GPS, but are afraid of getting lost, save your money and follow the telephone lines like I did in the Sahara. All electric lines and telephone poles lead somewhere, the sun comes up in the east and sets in the west, and water runs down hill. If in doubt, wait until another vehicle comes by and ask for directions. I've made four rides around the world without a GPS and Marco Polo managed pretty well also. You can purchase a lot of $3 maps and a compass for the price of an inexpensive GPS.

wrists. Very similar gloves are offered as motocross gloves. Both the bicycle and motocross gloves cost five times as much as very similar "contractor" gloves sold at larger home building supply stores.

Two riders traveling at the same speed rolling across Kansas on Interstate 70 are going to arrive at the same time, given the same gas tank size and fuel consumption rate, no matter what accessories they bring along.

Check to see if the spark plugs your motorcycle uses are sold at discount auto parts stores. One set of my plugs was five times more expensive at my local motorcycle shop than the car parts store.

If you have to replace a worn chain, replace the sprockets at the same time. A new chain will wear twice as fast on the used sprockets, and then you will need another one.

The ultimate way to save money on the wear and tear of your motorcycle is to haul it in the back of your pick-up truck or on a trailer to the rally you want to attend. This way you won't have to spend money on washing it to make it look pretty while touring around the rally; you won't wear out chains, sprockets, or tires; and you won't have to wear yourself out getting there and thus need an expensive room in which to heal. There are some budget savings when hauling motorcycles around behind cars and trucks, but usually the savings come when multiple motorcycles are hauled therefore spreading the cost of the vehicle hauling them over several riders.

Not having the most expensive equipment to make your tour does not mean you are going to fall off the face of the earth without it. A $1,000 laptop to read your planning program and download photographs from your $5,000 digital camera, with a $1,000 GPS, $1,000 CD player with changer, CB radio, satellite phone and radio, electronic roll chart, and needed battery chargers or battery packs are not going to make your tour any more physically comfortable than going without them, only more expensive. Two riders traveling at the same speed rolling across Kansas on Interstate 70 are going to arrive at the same time, given the same gas tank size and fuel

consumption rate, no matter what accessories they bring along.

While I am not a poverty motorcyclist, draining gas from gas pump hoses to get the extra drops or sponging off friends for meals and sleeping, I do like to live on a meager budget, trying to maximize the time I have for touring at the expense of giving away money for things I can live without. If you can wheelie out of your dealer's parking lot while yelling, "Send the bill to Harley-Davidson!" and your entourage on the payroll is following you, then do not bother with stretching your dollars. Maximize your riding. That's what the budget-conscious tourer is doing too.

This was an "ultimate budget tourer" for 'round the world riders. When the motorcycle came to a shore I suppose its owner proposed to load the bike and gear in the boat for the water crossing. I did once see two German travelers who had mounted their Yamaha XT motorcycles on a raft to propel a paddle wheel to navigate a length of the Yukon River, a cheap form of river transport.

PHYSICAL HAZARDS

Chapter 9

WHAT YOU WILL LEARN

• Strategies for dealing with traffic and other problems caused by fellow riders and drivers

• How to spot and adapt to changing road conditions

• Tips and strategies for avoiding animals, both dead and alive

Imagine trying to swerve around this boulder after dark. With few or no road crews, this bolder in Vietnam would probably lay on the road until some truck, car, or motorcycle ran into it at night. In a country with an estimated 40 million motorcycles, the odds were pretty high it would be a cycle rather than a car or truck.

There are hundreds of times each day you are at risk while touring, though often you do not realize how risky those situations are. Whether the risks involve animals in front of you or potholes in the road, not being prepared for them increases your chances of crashing as the result of making contact or trying to avoid them.

THE HUMAN ELEMENT

When people ask me what is the most dangerous touring I have done in my rides around the world, they are often surprised when I tell them that I-405 around Los Angeles scares me more than what many consider to be bad roads. That is because on I-405 it seems everyone is traveling at a high rate of speed, cutting in and out of traffic, and I am usually unprepared for the flow when I hit it.

India probably ranks as the most often designated "dangerous riding" country on the planet; however, it is Taiwan that has the highest incidence of traffic accidents involving motorcycles. In Thailand, during the Christmas and New Year's vacations, there are four deaths per hour on the highways, half of which involve motorcycles.

Whether the risks involve animals in front of you or potholes in the road, not being prepared for them increases your chances of crashing as the result of making contact or trying to avoid them.

The numbers are worse in Laos, and Cambodia does not seem to keep records. The high numbers are due to the large

Touring India I learned to expect anything on the road. Here the local farmers were using the cars and trucks to drive over their crop to separate the chaff from the wheat. Riding over this was tricky as the dried wheat was extremely slippery on the pavement.

numbers of motorcycles on the road, the lack of protective riding gear, poor road conditions, and bad drivers.

While I have ridden through all of these dangerous countries I always do so with my riding antenna up and my senses on high alert. It is when I get back to the United States that I find that if I do not force myself to keep aware, I am lulled into thinking our roadway systems are safe when they are not. Ask a tourer if he would consider making a tour through Colombia and he will probably say, "No, it's too dangerous." And yet, the "killingist city in the world" is Los Angeles. When I am in Colombia my senses are on high alert. When I am riding through Los Angeles, I am fooled into bliss by thinking it is safe because I am in America.

For instance, as I was riding on the I-405 recently I found myself noticing all of the trash that was piled up against the center median. Road rubbish, like aluminum ladders, lawn chairs, 50-gallon plastic garbage containers, and mattresses were lying there, usually smashed or bent. They had fallen off of some vehicle and landed on the roadway where they were eventually run over by some car or truck. While a car or truck driver might survive after hitting an aluminum lawn chair at 80 miles per hour, I think my odds of staying upright and alive after doing the same on a motorcycle are far less likely.

Each year in Brazil more people die on the roads than the United States lost in the Vietnam War, more than 50,000. A lot of them die from speed. As I was touring through Brazil, it seemed that every driver, whether in a truck or a car, had some racing blood in their veins. While going fast seemed to be a national sport, maintaining safe distances and good driving habits on bad roads did not. I remember watching a group of truck drivers at a truck stop chase their lunch with several bottles of strong

As the day wore on I did not realize my vision was becoming less clear from the collection of bugs on my face shield. These were Siberian mosquitoes, some of the meanest I had seen in the world. Several times I had to stop just to clean off my visor.

Each year in Brazil more people die on the roads than the United States lost in the Vietnam War.

Brazilian beer, then stumble back into the cabs of their trucks and back on to the roadway for an afternoon of bumper trucks and cars.

As I was riding across Russia one afternoon I realized I was hitting more potholes than usual and finally realized it was because I could not see them soon enough to avoid them. My usual miss rate is about 95 to 98 percent at speed, but that afternoon it had dropped to about 90 percent. I knew that sooner or later I was going to hit one hard enough to damage either my motorcycle or myself. I finally pulled over and stopped, trying to figure out why my usual roll and avoidance rate was off for the day. When I took my helmet off I found the reason I could not see was that the face shield had become clouded to the point of murkily limiting my vision.

The number one physical hazard you will face is that of a vehicle operated by another human being. I view all of them as a potential hazard, even when they are following behind me. Realistically, I know the largest exposure I have to harm is from a vehicle making a turn in front of me. However, while riding, my eyes are constantly roving, including a glance at my mirrors to see what or who is coming up behind me.

I have learned never to trust any vehicle in front of me. While touring Europe I discovered that many drivers are aware of the motorcycle following them and try to let them pass. This is usually manifested by their turning their right turn signal on and easing slightly to the right to allow room for the motorcycle to pass on the centerline, sometimes with a vehicle coming from the opposite direction.

Just about the time you think you have their system figured out and are comfortable splitting lanes is when you learn the exceptions to the rule, like when the car in front of you has turned on his right turn signal to make a right turn. While it may pull over slightly, the driver may decide at the last second that he or she needs a wider turning space and swing slightly out to the left, pushing you into the lane of the oncoming traffic. My personal rule for this physical hazard is that if a vehicle in front of you can make a turn, whether left or right, I do not trust it not to.

In Mexico and much of Latin and South America, the turn signal routine is just the reverse: A vehicle in front of you signals with the left turn signal that it is safe for you to pass. Sometimes the turn signal will be accompanied by the driver waving his hand up and down or encouraging you to make your pass, sometimes not. And sometimes when the car, truck, or bus has the signal on it means it's going to make a left turn in

As I came over a slight rise in the road, four camels that had been lying down on the road in front of me stood up. Rather than plow through the dromedary pack at 60 miles per hour, I rode into the ditch and ended up flying over the handlebars. Now I slow down as I approach rises in the road.

In India and Bangladesh crashed vehicles were often left on the roadway for weeks. Sometimes mechanics made repairs to the wrecked vehicles while they were on the road, leaving large oil pools after driving away.

front of you. The physical hazard of that happening has taught me never to trust what the vehicle in front of me is signaling. As in Europe, I will not pass a vehicle unless there are no roads, parking lots, or shoulder on the left it may turn into, and unless I see I have enough room to safely make the pass. More than once I have had trucks encourage me to pass only to find a vehicle coming at me in the opposite lane. It was explained to me that the truck drivers were probably just having a little fun to see how good of a driver I was, they were breaking up the monotony of their slow driving day, or they did not know I could not safely make the pass in the space they saw ahead. Whatever their reasons, I no longer trust them.

There are several good books on safe riding and riding techniques. Those by David Hough (*Proficient Motorcycling* and *Street Strategies*) and Lee Parks (*Total Control*) are among the best I have found of how the motorcycle is controlled and how to avoid various road hazards. While no book can prepare you for every possible hazard you might encounter, these form a good basis for how to manage your motorcycle.

As I rode out of New Delhi, India, early one morning I was "touched" or hit four

The number one physical hazard you will face is that of a vehicle operated by another human being.

Running over this snake in Brazil was like running over a greased inner tube half filled with sand. A second snake that I hit in Mexico was about the diameter of a copper pipe. Imagine a moving driveshaft lying across your lane. I've no love of snakes, dead or alive.

Cobblestones are fine when dry, just a bit bumpy as you ride over them. Wet, they can be like riding over ice cubes, especially the older ones that have been polished by centuries of vehicles passing over them. When wet, slow down and stay off the front brake, especially in turns or approaching intersections where oil droppings can make them even more slippery.

times by other vehicles, two coming from the opposite direction. I had just left Europe where cars, trucks, and buses seemed to regard motorcycles as equals on the road. In India the rules of the road changed considerably. The principal survival factor seemed to be the rule of he who has the biggest vehicle owns the road. There was no such thing as "my space" or "my lane." Trucks, cars, buses, even tractors were at home in my lane. If I did not yield, sometimes having to ride off the road, they would run over me. It was quite a surprise from having just left the Alps where cars would pull over to let me pass on my motorcycle.

Not surprisingly, at the top of the road hierarchy were cows, sacred animals. All vehicles would yield to cows and there was never honking when they meandered onto the pavement, whether in congested urban areas or in the countryside. At the bottom of the hierarchy were people and other animals. It was not unusual to see a careening bus highball through a crowded market, sending people and animals scrambling in all directions. As the bus approached the crowd the driver would start to honk the horn and continue honking until clear of the congestion.

The bus's number one tool for managing India roads in front of any vehicle is the horn. There are shops that specialize in installing the largest and loudest horn the vehicle owner can afford. This is true in Bangladesh, Nepal, as well as Pakistan. If you don't use your horn, the crowds that seem to live on the paved surfaces of this part of the world will not yield quickly to your oncoming vehicle.

ROAD CONDITIONS

Dark places on the road in front of you

I found a mix of rocks and straw on this road in Ecuador. I could easily pick my way through it during daylight hours, but I doubt I would have spotted it at night.

usually mean something is not right. The dark spots may be melting tar, like the tar snakes that partially fill the cracks on some roads. In hot weather, they become soft and very slippery, and your front and rear wheel can easily slide when passing over them. At other times the dark spots can signal oil on the road, or some other liquid or moisture that will make the surface slippery. Throughout many Third World countries it is not unusual for a broken vehicle to be repaired on the road. Often this means oil, gasoline, or diesel fuel is drained onto the road surface. When the vehicle is moveable it is driven off, but no one comes back and cleans the road surface. These dark spots can be as slippery as ice, especially when braking or in a curve.

In the Italian town of Cortina I felt the back wheel slide while riding slowly through an uphill right-hand curve on what appeared to be a safe corner in a light rain. I was so surprised that I circled around and tried the curve again to see if I could spot what on the road surface had made the curve so slippery. This time I used a different part of the lane so I could look at the one I had ridden in before and rode more slowly than before. The front wheel washed out this time, dumping me ungracefully on the pavement, albeit at a slow speed, in front of a few astonished pedestrians. After I righted my packed motorcycle with the help of several of the watchers who came to my rescue, I parked it and walked back to the corner. The entire lane was covered in a thin layer of diesel fuel, probably left there by a bus or truck that had topped off their tank at the station at the bottom of the hill. It was so fresh it had not had time to discolor the pavement and there was no way I could have seen it. My bad luck was riding over it shortly after it had sloshed out the overfilled tank. It was lucky I had been riding so slowly that my fall was at less than 5 miles per hour and there was nothing on the corner for me to slide into or under. My lesson was to slow down when passing a gas station at the bottom of a hill.

Early one misty morning I was riding on a twisting paved mountain road in Laos

when my back wheel slid out and I crashed. I was riding slow enough not to hurt my motorcycle or myself. Looking back at the curve I could see a dark patch on the pavement and concluded it was from oil dropped by cars and trucks. The mist had fogged my face shield so I concluded I had not seen the slippery stuff. Three turns later I crashed again, this time when the front wheel slid out. Again, nothing was hurt; however, I was not about to ride any farther until I could figure out what I was doing wrong. This time my face shield was clear and I still had not seen what was so slippery.

Stepping onto the road I slipped and fell down. Trying to stand up was like wearing ice skates, a flopping affair. Upon close up inspection I found oil-like black droppings from the overhanging trees covered the whole road. With the morning mist on top it made the pavement as slippery as if someone had oiled the curve. There was no discoloration to the pavement because the droppings were the same color as the tarred pavement surface. I had been lucky in that both times I crashed I had not been riding very fast due to the lack of visibility, and both times I low-sided and slid off the road onto the soft grassy shoulders. About the only thing that had been wounded was my ego.

Our egos often make road hazards more

No matter how powerful your headlight, touring at night is still a far more dangerous proposition than daytime touring. *Darwin Holmstrom*

There are some roads less traveled for a reason. A rainstorm had washed out this road in Arizona. I could have ridden around it, but foolishly followed a jeep. An unwritten rule for this kind of touring is "a fool and his motorcycle are soon parted."

Riders on heavily laden touring motorcycles ride too fast over these sections. Sometimes the soft gravel is 6 to 10 inches deep. When speeding motorcyclists hit these sections, rather than slow down to a crawl and paddle, they try to plow through it. The front wheel begins to wobble and the pilot soon finds himself struggling to stay on top of what can be likened to a 1,000-pound greased pig.

My ego has taken me over physical hazards that I knew were a mistake. In Brazil I came upon a group of trucks that were jammed up at the bottom of a greasy red mud road that went steeply uphill. I could see where several of the trucks had tried to drive up and had slid and slipped back down, contributing to the carnage at the bottom.

As I rode up to the crowd of truck drivers standing around one of the askewed trucks, they told me I should go ahead and ride up the hill. I told them that on my overweight motorcycle I doubted I could make the climb. They said it would be at least a day or two until the muddy stuff dried out or a road scraper came along and bladed it off to the sides and into the jungle below.

I looked at the tracks and doubted I could pick my way through the ruts and dry sections to the top, but the Brazilian truck drivers kept egging me on, saying a motorcycle could make it and I should have no

dangerous than they should be. Each year numerous motorcyclists crash on the Alaska Highway due to what is classified as excessive speed. They crash not on the paved sections but the slow-speed gravel sections that are common in construction zones. Sometimes these sections can be 10 miles in length and are found in a different place every year. The Alaska Highway is always under repair somewhere because the weather changes cause breakage and damage to the road surfaces.

I have learned to walk through murky waters like this before trying to ride through them. I once discovered there was a bridge underneath that dropped off rather deeply on each side. Another time I found a slick log about the size of a telephone pole lying at a 90-degree angle across my path.

problem being the long rider that I was. I remember one saying something like, "Of course you can make it, you're on a motorcycle." The little voice in the back of my head was quietly and rationally saying, "You can't make it, it is too steep and greasy," while the ego was wildly screaming, "Go ahead and show them what you can do."

I started up the hill at speed but had to back off as the front wheel wanted to go into tracks the back wheel did not want to follow. About halfway up the hill I could ride no further. The back wheel was spinning in the red mud and the front wheel was clogged up tight against the fork brace. I shut off the engine and tried to keep the motorcycle from sliding backwards down the hill. Nothing I did worked. The front wheel was locked, making my front brake efforts useless. I could not get my right foot onto the rear brake because I needed it on the ground to keep me from falling over. Next I was sliding backwards, gaining momentum, and trying frantically to keep the motorcycle upright with both feet sliding like outriggers. And upright I was as I sailed off the slipped track back-

wards and through the trees to the jungle floor below. I remember yelling an obscenity as I flew through the air, more at my ego than out of fear.

Somehow I ended up with my face in the soft dirt of the moist jungle floor, my face shield up and its opening stuffed with rotten leaves, muck, and dirt. I was pinned under the motorcycle. As my consciousness returned I could feel my legs being pulled. It was several of the

My ego has taken me over

physical hazards that I

knew were a mistake.

truckers. I believe they thought I was dead and were trying to get my pants off, hopefully to search for my money. However, knowing they were Brazilian, and truckers, and far away from the favors of their ladies, I later worried they had other notions in mind.

I startled them when I moved and they stopped tugging on my pants and stood up.

Believe what road signs say; they are there for a reason. This one was warning of hippos crossing the road, something I laughed at until I remembered the number of deer crossing signs I had seen in America and the dead deer shortly thereafter.

Deer are probably the number one animal enemy of motorcyclists. Each year there are more stories of motorcyclists running into deer, and most often they are sad stories. The closest I have come to hitting one was touching a tail with the end of my handlebar one night in Colorado, and I never even saw it standing in the middle of the road.

As I worked the jungle goo out of my mouth and eyes, I motioned them to help me get out from under the motorcycle. They grabbed the motorcycle and lifted it off me. Fortunately, I had broken no bones.

We spent the afternoon sweating and struggling to get the motorcycle out of the jungle and back to the mud road, then down to the parked trucks at the bottom. My lesson was to realize some physical hazards are best avoided and to ignore my motorcyclist ego when someone says, "But you're a biker," or "But you're riding a motorcycle."

FOREIGN OBJECTS, FOREIGN LANDS

Most often you are trying to avoid things in or around the road in front of you that can cause you to crash. When I saw a manhole in my riding lane missing a manhole cover in Panama, I desperately tried to avoid the void. Thieves during a heavy rainstorm had removed the cover. With the flooded sewer system and foot-deep water on the street, car drivers would not be able to see the gaping hole and avoid driving into it, blowing out the tire and bringing the vehicle to a stop.

I have learned to slow down whenever I see an animal on the side of the road. A number of times they have made sudden dashes in front of my motorcycle. While this one in South America was "fixed," it still slowed me down enough as I approached to cause me to stop and take a photograph.

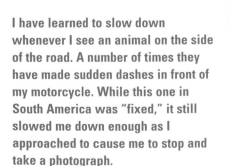

The thieves would then rush to the disabled vehicle and rob the driver. I had nearly ridden into the open manhole not expecting to find this kind of road hazard.

Animals, dead or alive, may be the second biggest physical hazard to avoid while touring. In New Zealand, a country with some of the most perfect touring roads in the world, a major road hazard is the numerous road-killed possums. Interstate 80 across Pennsylvania is littered with road-killed deer. In the outback of Australia, kangaroos litter the road like 100-pound bags of potatoes. I have seen armadillos the size of basketballs laying in my path across Texas and Oklahoma, thousands of frogs splattered by trucks on Interstate 10 across Louisiana, spoiling sheep and horses in Arizona, and a road-killed moose as big as a horse taking up one lane in British Colombia.

Animals, dead or alive, may be the second biggest physical hazard to avoid while touring.

Here are some rules on how to avoid dead animals in the road:

• Slow down when approaching them, there might be something alive feeding on them that will scoot in front of or spook you.

• Expect the unexpected on blind curves. An 800-pound lump of fur that was prime rib on the hoof until a truck hit it takes up a full driving lane and an oncoming vehicle can take up the other.

• Do not tailgate or follow other vehicles too closely, stay in their tire tracks, not the middle of the lane. They can clear a road kill that will quickly appear at speed under the rear of their vehicle, and if too close, you will not have enough time to avoid it.

• Do not ride at night. You may never see that dark dead lump in the road in front of you.

More deadly than dead animals are the live ones. Deer and dogs are probably the biggest hazards in the live animal category. There is seldom anything you can do, other

While touring Montana this snake sped across the road in front of me. I skidded over it, which flipped it up into the wheelwell of my Indian Chief. On another occasion a similar experience had the snake flapping against my rear lower leg. The Chief, with its valanced rear fender, kept the snake from getting to me.

Road obstacles come in many shapes and colors. In Vietnam, where there is little money for road signs to keep drivers from driving on new sections of tarred road, they merely make it impossible by placing tire-cutting or accident-causing rocks in your path.

My rule for animals on or along roads, including the two-legged ones, is never trust them.

than slow down, to avoid hitting them when they want to cross traffic.

Some motorcyclists believe in mounting deer whistles on their bikes to scare deer away from their moving motorcycles. Others believe in carrying a lucky talisman. Both work as well as radar jammers or treasure maps to the Lost Dutchman's Mine.

I started one of my world tours aiming to tag the northernmost point on the North American continent I could ride to, Deadhorse, Alaska. Riding on a gravel road on the way up through a small village in the Yukon, a large dog ran full speed into my front wheel. It came from a 90-degree angle and never slowed down. The dog was on a mission to die, and did, but failed in its mission to take me with it. I crashed hard, breaking numerous parts on the motorcycle I had to ride the rest of the way around the world. Because of some Buddhist good karma, and the fact I was wearing the full-protection body armor in my riding suit, I only suffered some bruises. While I am a dog lover, I hated the one that knocked me down, so much so that I took a piece of it with me. That piece is still glued to my front fender, maybe having brought me more good joss because that was the last dog I hit on that ride touring the globe.

My rule for animals on or along roads, including the two-legged ones, is never trust them. If they are in striking range I assume they are going to make an effort to run into

What looks to be a rock in the road was actually a large turtle. Hitting it at speed would have had the same effect as a rock. At night I doubt I would have seen it in my path.

or in front of me. I give them a wide berth and slow down when approaching them. Like a random atom, they can zip in any direction, and too often I have had them zip at me on my motorcycle.

Animals, dead or alive, junk in the road, bad roads, speed bumps, ice, mud, and numerous other physical hazards in front of me can often be avoided if I can see them in time, which means during daylight hours. Touring after it becomes dark changes the whole strategy.

One night I rode 70 miles per hour into a flock of brown birds that were standing on the road. I never saw them until one smashed through my plastic windscreen and tried to push me off the back of the motorcycle. I know it was brown because when I stopped it was pinned against my chest. If you think your windscreen is going to protect you, have a baseball pitcher throw a 2 pound rock at it from 10 feet away. Some windshields might deflect it, but others will crack as mine did. I was lucky it did not slice my head off as it whizzed by.

I do a lot of night driving, but only in an automobile. Inside the cage and behind the windshield I am far safer from road hazards than I am on two wheels at the same speed. I knew this in my early riding years, but I was in youthful denial. After numerous close calls and some nighttime crashes, I limited my after-dark riding to what I considered good or safe roads, but I cranked up the candlepower of my lighting systems. However, after some

After some near-misses on global rides, I have made "Never ride after dark" my No. 1 Rule for Riding in Third World or developing countries.

near-misses on global rides, I have made "Never ride after dark" my No. 1 Rule for Riding in Third World or developing countries.

At the same time, I have added more wattage and lights to my motorcycle lighting

Rule No. 1 in touring any developing country is: Never Ride At Night. Rounding this corner in Mexico I was only able to scrub off a few miles per hour before slipping and sliding over the mud. After dark I would have never seen it and would have probably been found in the jungle below.

Lighting up the objects in front of you after dark has definite advantages if you are going to ride at night. This motorcycle had enough extra candlepower to brighten the road several times more than the stock light. After more than 1 million miles of riding, I've decided no amount of lighting is going to make riding after dark safe and I have quit doing it.

A few hours of comfort and laughter just do not balance the scale against the risk of riding after dark.

NIGHT AND DAY

Animals, dead or alive, junk in the road, bad roads, speed bumps, ice, mud, and numerous other physical hazards in front of me can often be avoided if I can see them in time, which means during daylight hours. Touring after it becomes dark changes the whole strategy.

systems, bought night riding glasses, and added good luck charms to my personal medicine bundle in the hopes of reducing the risk of running into or over something after dark. After hitting a deer one night while driving my car and nearly dying, I thought, "What if I had been on the motorcycle?" That was the last time I planned any nocturnal motorcycle riding. Not only am I fatigued after riding during the day, and my reflexes are slow, I can no longer balance the risk of riding a motorcycle after dark against the return.

Say my return was to spend the night swilling with friends and sleeping in their guestroom. I could not balance that pleasure against never seeing them again or maiming myself. A few hours of comfort and laughter just do not balance the scale against the risk of riding after dark. I will call friends I can't reach before dark and make plans to meet them for breakfast or move the day of my arrival if it works. If it does not, I will promise next time to leave earlier in the morning so I can ride in before dark. If my tour plan has me riding after dark, unless it is an absolute emergency, I abandon the plan and stop riding early.

A monster headlight on this Kawasaki KLR could light up the road in front of you well enough. One long-distance rider had max candlepower like this as he was passing a truck, enough to fully illuminate the deer that dashed in front of the semi just before the motorcycle collided with it. I suspect the rider's eyes got as big as the top light on this bike as he saw the deer.

I have also slowed my touring pace. Where I once raced from point A to point B, riding at velocities pushing the envelope of speed limits, and sometimes breaking them, I now try to smell the roses a bit more in my touring. I learned that it's not how fast I can ride through life, it's how long I can ride. When I feel the need to go fast, I load up my race bike and head for a road race track to compete or ride a track day. On the track, I am riding during daylight hours, all the traffic is moving in the same direction, the pavement is (usually) clean, and there are safe get-off areas for the times when speed exceeds my capability.

SURVIVAL ON THE ROAD

WHAT YOU WILL LEARN

- Dealing with law enforcement and other authorities

- Anticipating risk and danger and planning your trip accordingly

- Getting back on the road after accidents, medical emergencies, or theft

How good is your motorcycle insurance? Before starting out for a ride to Alaska find out if your insurance is any good in Canada. It most likely is not. You will also discover your roadside assistance plan is equally shallow. To get your wrecked motorcycle trucked off the Dalton Highway can easily cost you $1,500, and another $1,500 to get back home. I no longer take motorcycles outside of the country unless I can afford to leave them in another country, wrecked, stolen, or impounded.

Survival on the road means not only staying alive but also doing so with some comfort. Unless you are entered in a rally or race around the United States or the world, your plan should be flexible enough to allow for slippage or cancellation altogether.

Once I was several days into a group ride with two others across Europe and Asia that promised to pay for itself. The others were picking up the cost of my hotel sleeping because they did not want to camp, and two magazines had agreed to pay for stories about the three of us and our comparative motorcycles. The bottom line was my ride would essentially not cost me anything. The carrot for me was their offer to pay for a private room during the section we would cross by train. For a budget-conscious traveler like myself, the promise of going first class on a motorcycle ride was a dream come true. Instead of riding in a cattle car across the steppes of Russia, I pictured myself hoisting chilled vodka drinks in a

clean glass in the club car while watching the scrub trees roll by, sleeping nightly between fresh sheets, watching CNN or the BBC evening news in the hotel bars, and there would be money in the bank when I finished instead of being indebted to my credit card company.

The definition of the word adventure includes the word risk.

The dream nearly became a nightmare when my companions voted to turn around and go back home when uncertainty loomed about the condition of the road ahead and a failing charging system on one of their bikes meant they would have to be switching batteries between bikes daily over the coming weeks. With very little cash in a country where credit

One rider is saying, "Mike, the bike's not charging." The other, scratching his head, is trying to figure out how many days it is back to the nearest BMW repair shop. Carrying replacement electrical parts are part of your planning process if touring far away from your nearest supply center.

cards were seldom taken, I was faced with turning tail as well or changing my plans for the three-week ride ahead.

I admit to liking the challenges of the unknown, solving problems like what to eat when I only had enough money to pay for gas, or how to solve a break down in a country where I knew only four or five words of the language. As I headed off on my own I knew there were some risks, potentially big ones, but risk is what makes adventure.

ADVENTURE AND RISK

Adventure is probably one of the most abused and violated words in the motorcycle travel spirit. The definition of the word adventure includes the word risk. Yet many motorcyclists are sold an adventure when, in fact, the sellers remove as much of the risk as possible. For instance, look at how many of the organized tours use the word *adventure* in their marketing when the major draw is for you to have as little risk as possible. Risk avoidance is why these adventure tours are so popular, especially to fearsome Americans. With a tour guide riding in front of you and a chase truck following you, your group ducking into and out of gated hotels at night, about the biggest risk you experience is not finding an ATM or a special souvenir for those back home.

At the other end of the spectrum are the real adventure riders, mostly Europeans,

those out there flying without a safety net, totally self-sufficient and dependent on their ability to face risk and avoid disaster. Their wits, skills, and intuition allow them to enjoy real adventure by managing the risks, not by paying someone else to remove or manage risk for them.

As I rode into the unknown for three weeks of riding solo across Russia, into places many were afraid to go, even in the protection of a car or train, I felt I would survive, having confidence in my traveling skills and decision-making ability. I do admit I did have some concerns about

The next best thing to taking a full-on guided tour is to make your own guided tour with your personal driver and truck following you. That is what this motorcyclist was doing when I met him crossing Russia. Had I been with him my only worry would have been what to do if the truck broke down.

When I came to a nearly impassable section of swamp in Siberia, rather than wait for a truck to come along to carry me across, I paid to have it packed into a cargo car. I then paid a little "black money" under the table to the train employees to let me ride in the cargo car with the motorcycle, one of the more fun and memorable parts of my tour across Russia.

eating, but knew I could afford to loose some 20 to 40 pounds if I had to.

Looking back on my adventure, the memory of days riding without eating to save money have dimmed, as have the nights sleeping on the frozen tundra in my tent instead of in warm, dry hotel rooms. I can now laugh at how the scrub trees looked through the slats of the smelly cargo car while I sipped free bootleg vodka from a bottle instead of from a crystal glass while sitting on the plush seats of a club car. While

having been abandoned and forced to go alone could have been a nightmare, in the end it was one of my more memorable adventures. Not only did I meet and taste some parts of a culture I would have undoubtedly missed in hotels or riding in a first-class sleeper, I also got rid of 30 pounds of excess body baggage. It was a great tour and if I could, I would do it exactly the same way again, except for the three to four days I had to ride while sick to keep to a timeline forced by the government due to my visa requirements. My plans were flexible, but those of the government were not.

LAW ENFORCEMENT AND OTHER AUTHORITIES

I once took a riding companion through Nepal and committed to getting her down to Bangladesh and then across India because she was afraid to ride through those countries alone. Our getting out of Bangladesh was delayed because she spent days sending and answering e-mail she felt was more important than her expiring visa. When I asked her how she was going to deal with it being expired when we exited Nepal she said she had a plan for the border officials rather than trying to get it extended in Kathmandu again.

She said that if her plan did not work I could wait for her on the India side while she

When the police pull you over in some countries they are serious about giving you a ticket for a moving violation. Other times they are only collecting money as a "road tax." I am always friendly, take off my helmet and sunglasses, and never offer a bribe until it is clear that is what is being asked for.

LUCK

Lost or stolen items, ranging from motorcycles to credit cards, can halt a tour or turn it into a nightmare. While riding across Wyoming, my wallet unknowingly worked its way out of my riding jacket, thanks in part to manipulations by a pillion trying to be helpful by giving me an unwanted back and shoulder rub. Inside the wallet were all my credit cards and the usual important papers like motorcycle registration, proof of insurance, driver's license, folding money, and membership cards. Its loss was a disaster.

I could remember seeing it when I last paid for gas, so we rode back 100 miles on Interstate 80 trying to see if it was laying on the pavement on the other side of the road. No wallet had been turned in at the gas station, so I retraced my steps again, but darkness was faster than I was. I borrowed $50 for a motel room and vowed to look again at first light.

Not having the credit cards and no one to call at home for credit card numbers and emergency telephone numbers meant I would have to kill the cards if I couldn't find them. I crossed my fingers and took the chance the wallet was on the highway and not in the hands of someone who would use what they found inside.

In the morning I found the wallet, laying face up and open, two $100 bills partially exposed, on the far right painted line. Trucks and cars had passed it all night long, but not one had run over it. From that point forward I vowed never to carry all my credit cards in one place and never to put my wallet in a pocket that did not Velcro or zip closed while riding.

In my wallet I carry one medical alert card with the name of my insurer and medical evacuation company. I also carry a second set of cards in one of my riding jacket pockets. This way if someone steals my wallet at a crash scene and I am not conscious, attendants can find the other cards if they look through my pockets.

I had a small crash here in Taiwan, nothing scratched or broken. However, in case of serious injury I wear medical ID tags with a telephone number to call in the United States as well as my blood type, name, and religion. It's cheap insurance.

would ride back to Kathmandu and pay for another extension. While my plan was flexible it seemed to be tied to hers no matter what.

At the border I cleared Customs and Immigration, then waited for her outside with the motorcycles as she entered the offices. Fifteen minutes went by before she came out, wiping tears from her face. I asked if she was OK, and she said she was.

Once we cleared the India side she explained that the Nepal officials had demanded she pay an extra $150 for having overstayed her visa. She told them she did not have the $150 and when they told her to get it from her friend, meaning me, she said I was not a friend, only someone who had reached the border at the same time. Then she said she started to cry. The officials took

Crashing happens. If your back-up plan for this kind of accident is your cell phone and 911, you need to stay close to home. There are still many places in the United States with no cell service and 911 can be hours away.

My life was nearly ended when an oncoming car swerved to avoid a crashing truck and drove into my lane. That's my motorcycle halfway up the hill. Had I been hit or killed in this South American country, most likely it would have been my fault. Their legal system is based on Napoleonic Law, which says you are guilty until you prove yourself innocent. Since I may not have been around to prove my innocence, I would have been found guilty.

pity on her for having no money and no friend and told her she could go. I said I was surprised she could cry so easily. She laughed and told me she could turn her tears on and off as easily as turning the spigots on a sink.

My plan for the same problem would have never involved crying. First, I know I could not work up alligator tears on call, and second, I very much doubt the male government officials would take pity on a crying man in their office and waive their rules. I believe my plan would have involved

paying the money; the question would be how much.

When I am stopped by any law enforcement official I am a "Yes sir, no sir" person. While I do not like to yield to their authority, I know there is nothing to win by not doing so, and possibly some gain if I do.

While we foolishly think the locks on the boxes will keep a thief out, imagine how quickly a crow bar could pry a top or side open.

I pull over, take off my helmet, sunglasses, gloves, and pull out my earplugs. I do not start digging in my jacket for my wallet (which could as easily be a gun, for all they know) until I am asked to, then I tell the guard what I am reaching for. I never make an offer for a bribe and generally yield to the fact I must have been doing something wrong. When I am told it was speeding, I do not try to debate it by the side of the road because I have seldom won those debates. What I have been able to do, by being naïve Mr. Harvey Milquetoast, is have the level dropped to where it is more affordable.

Another near miss in Africa. The driver of the car swerved coming at me, then rolled the car coming down my lane. No amount of rider training can prepare you for this type of accident. Good medical evacuation insurance will send a jet to bring you to your home hospital, or return your remains.

In foreign countries I pretend I do not understand a word the officer is saying and stumble along presenting the image of the stupid tourist. Once, while stopped in Argentina, it took me nearly an hour to talk my way down from a $400 fine to $25 by pleading I did not have the $400, only the $25 I was showing the officer that I carried in my throw-down wallet, the wallet I was able to lose.

In Panama I was flagged down by an officer stopped on the side of the road who demanded $25, saying I was speeding. As

Santiago, Chile, where he planned on spending his vacation riding before shipping it and himself back to California. When he arrived in Santiago and went to pick up his motorcycle it was not there, but in Brazil. After several days of waiting and it never arriving he rented a car for his tour and spent some memorable days seeing Chile and Argentina. He and his motorcycle were eventually reunited in Los Angeles. While his original plan failed, it was flexible enough to let him enjoy some of his vacation.

If you can't pick up your bike when it falls over, turn off the gas immediately. Gas running into the carburetor can flow freely into a cylinder and down into the crankcase. Once the bike is righted it is possible to bend the connecting rods or valves with a cylinder full of gas, or to drive off with oil contaminated or diluted by gasoline.

Having an accident while touring is the major nightmare of surviving on the road.

he had no radar or VASCAR his estimate of my speed was a guess and I knew the ticket was more of a road tax than a fine for breaking the law. We settled on a $5 fine after haggling and smiling at each other for ten minutes while I looked at his motorcycle and he looked at mine.

A friend once crated and paid for his motorcycle to be flown from Los Angeles to

Can you pick up your own motorcycle when it falls over? You might want to learn how by practicing somewhere soft before heading out on the highway, especially if traveling alone. I could lever this monster BMW up only once or twice in an afternoon. Fully loaded it weighed close to 800 pounds, which is 700 more than I can lift on a good day.

CRASHES, FALLS, AND OLD FASHIONED CLUMSINESS

Having an accident while touring is the major nightmare of surviving on the road. We try to ignore the possibility, deny that it

will happen to us, and yet each year thousands of motorcyclists are hurt or killed while riding away from home.

I am always surprised at how little time travelers put into planning for the possibility of a crash. In part I think it's ego overriding common sense for them not to think they might make a riding mistake and crash, that they are 100 percent competent. Of course this is foolishness because it fails to take into account those accidents that are not the fault of the motorcyclists, those that can't be avoided.

One of my traveling friends knows that if her motorcycle falls over she cannot pick it up. Her plan for when it happens is quite simple: she depends on others to come to her rescue. Sometimes she says it is only a matter of seconds; other times she has had to wait for hours. One of the stories she tells is of when her motorcycle fell over in Africa when there was no one around. She says she turned off the ignition and gas, then took off her hot

I carry several sets of latex gloves. They fold up small and can be used for more than dealing with blood. In this photo, a physician who was on our tour came equipped with everything he needed to suture a gash. The procedure was preformed deftly on top of an outdoor table outside the motel room in Alaska 200 miles from the nearest clinic or hospital.

riding jacket and helmet, then dug out her umbrella. It was a humorous surprise for the truckload of village natives when they came upon her sitting under her umbrella next to her horizontal motorcycle in the deep sand of the desert, miles from anywhere and anyone. She said it would have been perfect for a book or magazine cover.

My motorcycle once fell over in a stream, dumping the open tank bag contents into the stream. While I was hurriedly trying to save my film and cameras from floating downstream I let the motorcycle lay. Unbeknownst to me, gasoline was flowing out the top of the gas tank and downstream. I calmly took several photos of the flopped bike before I realized what my bike was doing to the pristine stream. I rushed over to it and tried to right it, but the weight of the luggage and the soft rock streambed made lifting it impossible. I frantically tore off the luggage and threw it on shore, then was able to get the bike upright.

When I am doing some of my more extreme touring, whether off road or well away from urban areas, I carry a large can of spaghetti in case of an emergency.

After I got the motorcycle up and started, I rode it to the shore where I repacked and cursed my stupidity for calmly taking photographs while my precious fuel ran out. What fuel was left in the gas tank was not enough to get me out of the wilderness and to the next fuel supply. I decided to ride as far as I could, looking for a safe place to spend the night away from the bears. The next day a fisherman drove by in a jeep and I was able to talk him out of half a gallon of gas, all I needed to get back to the pavement and a nearby gas station. The half-gallon was what I had lost while trying to get the motorcycle upright. If I had been able to pick it up without unpacking it

RIDING WITH OTHERS

While your riding may be worry- and crash-free, there is always the possibility that your touring pal or pillion might need some help. I try to work out a system of communication with my pillion that does not use words. I tell them to hit me twice on the back, arms, or shoulders if they need to stop. When that happens I will pull over as soon as it is safe, like into a gas station or restaurant parking lot. They should use this signal if they need a toilet soon, or they are starting to cramp up and need to walk around.

The second signal I give them is to hit me hard three times. This means "STOP IMMEDIATELY!" This could be an emergency, like a bag having fallen off the back of the motorcycle or a foreign object in their eye. Or they see something wrong with the motorcycle I cannot, like a side cover about to work loose or a bag strap trying to get tangled in a wheel.

When you or your riding buddies are hurt, someone should know CPR. It takes only a few hours to take a CPR course before going on a tour. Knowing CPR and some medical basics may well save your life or the life of someone you meet.

I would not have had the memorable evening in an abandoned cabin sharing the floor with rats, mice, and mosquitoes, but no bears.

EMERGENCY GEAR

I carry a large medical kit with me when I tour. Some would argue it is too large, but I know what I have needed and used in the past. My kit includes bandages, sutures,

Do not be afraid to try the local remedies for pulled or sore muscles. I could not pass up this rest stop after having banged a knee on a car bumper one afternoon.

At first I thought this was a top box on the back of the motorcycle. Then I realized it was a saddlebag. The rider had crashed, ripping off both aluminum panniers. His back-up plan was his two riding buddies. They split the goods that he was carrying in his one bag that was destroyed. His explanation for the crash? "Dunno, maybe too much power into the curve."

syringes, and several forms of prescription drugs for everything from pain to malaria. Once, when crossing the border into Chile, my medical kit was carefully inspected by the customs official. When finished, one commented, "You have the whole pharmacy in here." And I had the letters and prescriptions from my physicians to prove I legally could carry them. The only thing better would have been to have my physician with me.

While traveling in Laos I was following a pair of local boys who were riding two-up on a 110-cc Suzuki when they missed a curve

and crashed. The passenger flew over the top of the driver and landed on his head while the pilot was able to hang on suffering only scrapes and scratches. The passenger had some pretty good lumps, but the helmet had saved his head. His major injury was he had bitten through his tongue and it was bleeding profusely. It also was hurting him terribly.

They told me the nearest town and clinic was only about 10 miles away, so I knew he would not bleed to death in the time it would take to get him there. What I wanted to do was try and slow the bleeding and reduce his pain, leaving the sewing work to the local medic or physician. I dug out my medical kit and some painkillers. I smashed the pills to powder. With my latex gloves on I worked the powder into the holes in his tongue, then had him wash down what was left of the pain powder with a swallow of vodka. He did not like my holding his tongue with one hand while smearing it with the pain powder with the other, but all the while his eyes were on the bottle of vodka. He tried to go for a second swig of vodka before I could get the bottle away from him. I figured at his size, about 100 pounds, two painkillers and a swig of vodka would be enough not to feel any pain, but I did not want to take the chance a second hit of 40-proof might have at stopping his heart.

He could not speak English and I could not speak Laotian, but he was able to communicate how thankful he was by clamping his hands together and bringing them to his head as he bowed slightly, a Buddhist sign of thanks and respect. He made the same sign again after pointing to the flask of vodka as I was putting it away.

When I am doing some of my more extreme touring, whether off road or well away from urban areas, I carry a large can of spaghetti in case of an emergency. If I can't find a restaurant or market before my riding day ends, I can open the can and have a cold meal that is better than no meal. I wash it down with the water I carry, and then have a nightcap with my small bottle of medicinal vodka. I have also used the vodka to sterilize things as well as a cleaning fluid, but it works best if ingested after a day of things going wrong.

THEFT AND LOSS

Theft insurance for your motorcycle may give you some sense of security but will seldom be enough money to replace what you have invested in it. Accessory items may be outside the limits of the policy. One option is to purchase special travel insurance that covers items like cameras, laptop computers, and other expensive items.

My personal form of theft insurance is to not carry expensive items. I have never carried a laptop computer or CD player on any of my four rides around the world. The cameras I carried were not top-of-the-line, but they were items that I carefully

My personal form of theft insurance is to not carry expensive items.

guarded. When I would leave my hotel room with the cameras in it, I would hide them on top of closets or hang one in the shower. The point was to keep them out of sight and not keep them together, hoping that if one were found the thief might think that was all I had.

The one time I had someone try to take one of my cameras was when a policeman stopped me at a roadside check point in Honduras. He was examining my camera case and pulled one out, then told me he would keep it because I had two and only

needed one. I grabbed it back. He tripped as I did so, and fell backwards on to the ground. His partner turned in time to see him fall and thought I had pushed him. When he started to reach for his gun I took it away from him. That cost me a night in a dark ugly jail for assaulting a police officer and I vowed to let the next one have the camera, as well as never to return to Honduras.

Sometimes your homeowner's insurance policy will cover items stolen while you are traveling. This is nice coverage if you have it, but you need to keep a record of serial numbers and receipts for the items you are taking. This option may not apply to certain items if they are taken outside the country.

Fifteen miles into the jungle of northern Thailand I dropped the motorcycle, which I was able to eventually pick up. I was able to rig the broken front brake lever with a pair of Vise-Grips I carried in my toolkit. My self-made toolkit carries more tools and spares than I will probably ever use, but like a Boy Scout I like to be prepared.

When things go wrong you should have someone you can call for help or advice. While the Internet has blanketed much of the world, it is still not the answer to everything. Take a good calling card with you when you travel and alert friends and co-workers that you may need to reach them for help or arranging for parts to be shipped to you.

When lost, do not panic. The world is a small enough place that sooner or later someone will come along. It might be an hour or a day, but you will only confuse yourself more by panicking. Here in the deep sand I was comforted by the numerous tire tracks.

replaced by a nice $20 watch and quietly rests in a safe place.

GETTING LOST

Some travelers panic when they get lost, feeling they need to know exactly where they are at all times, whether through their electronic GPS tether or a map. Others get frantic when turned around in a strange city or get diverted off a main street by a detour or traffic accident. It is best during these times to relax and tell yourself you are not really lost, just seeing something you would not have seen if the opportunity had not presented itself.

Sometimes your homeowner's insurance policy will cover items stolen while you are traveling.

If you are going to ask directions on how to get out of town when disoriented or lost, take directions with some caution. If you were headed west and your guide is pointing east ignore them. In many countries, like those of Latin America, if the person does not understand where you want to go they won't tell you. Instead they will try not to appear ignorant.

Generally, if I have a breakdown I try not to leave the motorcycle sitting alone by the

I used to wear an expensive Rolex watch when touring, having been told by another experienced traveler that if I were thrown in a foreign jail or prison, I would be able to purchase better food and medical supplies with links from the watch. I later found out the watch was not covered by homeowner's or traveler's insurance, so if it had been stolen it would be a big loss. About the same time I also awoke to the fact that in many of the countries where I was traveling I was a walking target with the watch, virtually saying "here is $12,000, right here on my wrist, all you or your buddies have to do is poke a knife or a gun in my stomach and it is yours." The Rolex has been

A bent beemer gets a ride home in the back of a pick-up truck. I have packed broken bikes into taxicabs, onto airplanes, and pulled one behind a horse once, slowly. One broken BMW rider found that it was cheaper, about half the price to fly his dead motorcycle down to Anchorage from Prudhoe Bay than it was to have it towed on a trailer behind a wrecker to Fairbanks.

My dream was to ride my motorcycle around the island of Zanzibar. When I got to the boat dock in Dar es Salaam I was told that the ferries to the island only carried people. The freighters did not carry people, only cargo. I paid these ten workers to lift my motorcycle onto the bow of the people ferry, then paid ten more at Zanzibar to unload it. I was able to travel with my motorcycle, thereby reducing possible theft or loss of parts.

side of the road while I go for help. One of my friends did that with his BMW when he ran out of gas on Interstate 70 going through Ohio. When he returned with a 2-gallon container of gas the fully loaded motorcycle was gone. It was reported that a pick-up truck had stopped and several men were seen loading the motorcycle into the back. Most people driving by assumed one of the men owned the motorcycle. It was never recovered, nor was it insured.

When I was told I would have to leave my motorcycle parked and unattended in a questionable warehouse in Dar es Salaam, I thought my plan to tour Zanzibar had been wrecked. I would not leave my motorcycle and much of my gear where it could be taken. Instead, I adjusted my plan and moved on. Flexibility is the key to survival.

If you are going to ask directions on how to get out of town when disoriented or lost, take directions with some caution.

MAKING A SURVIVAL KIT

By Lee Klancher

One of the simplest things you can do to prepare for emergencies is to put together a basic survival kit. This kit will allow you to build a shelter, build a fire, and signal for help. Should things go wrong on a tour, you'll be prepared.

- Portable bivvy/shelter
- Waterproof match safe
- Flashlight
- Fire starters
- Signal mirror
- Police whistle
- Parachute cord (50')
- Aluminum foil (2 pieces, 36" x 12")
- Insect repellant
- Water purification tablets
- The *Pocket Survival Guide*
- Compass

This list was compiled with reference to *The Pocket Survival Guide* by J. Wayne Fears and *Keller's Outdoor Survival Guide* by William Keller.

MAKING FRIENDS:
TALES FROM THE ROAD

Chapter 11

WHAT YOU WILL LEARN

- The real joy of motorcycle touring: Meeting new people and making new friends

- Keeping in touch after your tour is over

- How to deal with "being noticed"

I made friends with this man from a small village in the high Atlas Mountains of Morocco. He wanted his picture taken with my motorcycle in it and I agreed, but only if he would wear some stickers from Aerostich/Riderwearhouse and their Ride to Work Day. Happily he posed, then asked for two more stickers, which I gave him.

CHRISTMAS IN THAILAND

Rich and I were preparing similar Kawasaki motorcycles for our tours around the world. A mutual sponsor connected us through the Internet and suggested we meet in Seattle. Rich rode down from Vancouver and I came in from Denver.

Both of us are gearheads, so our evening was spent huddled together talking about modifications we had made to our motorcycles and lightly arguing why one plan was superior to the other. We also discussed our riding gear, choice of touring style, and common acquaintances. Our proposed routes were exchanged, and we agreed to keep in touch as we worked our way around the globe. My tour was planned to be much faster than his, five months for me and nearly two years for him, but we would be riding over some of the same routes through Africa, Europe, and Asia.

He was coming out of Africa just as I was about to enter. Going opposite directions we met in a campground in Spain where we spent two days together working on our motorcycles, trading news and tales from the road. We thought our paths might possibly cross again in Germany, which they did. Again, we spent hours talking about our motorcycles, routes we had taken, women, and memorable experiences we had touring similar parts of the globe. Afterwards we both departed for Russia, but at far different paces and on different vectors.

Upon parting we expected not to see each other again as I was on a fast ride across Europe and Asia while he was planning a much slower and more circuitous route. He was also trying to juggle his touring schedule with that of a lady friend. We promised to keep in touch. After I crossed Russia I sent him the name of friends I had made along the way in case he needed help or contacts when he followed parts of my route.

When I finished my five-month global tour he was still poking around in Europe.

Rather than spend a dreary winter snow-bound in Montana I decided to return to the Golden Triangle area and explore some small roads and trails I had missed on an earlier ride. Rich wrote that he too would be in some of the same countries I wanted to

One of the shows featured ladies performing various physical acts on a customized motorcycle that was lowered from the ceiling.

explore and there was a possibility that our paths would intersect again. I told him I would be spending the winter touring some remote areas in Laos, Burma, and Thailand where he too hoped to ride.

Both of our schedules were loose so we could not suggest any target dates. To complicate matters, access to the Internet to exchange messages was limited. We both knew we would find ourselves passing through Bangkok within a

window of two weeks, but were unsure of the exact dates. I wrote him which hotel I would be staying in, but advised it would only be for two nights, and then I would be back into the jungles near the Burmese border where there would be little chance for contact. When I arrived in Bangkok I checked for messages from Rich, found none, and assumed he had not been able to move as quickly as he had planned, having to cross several countries with uncertain borders.

I decided to take a friend to Bangkok's famous Patpong District for shopping and a few shows. One of the shows featured ladies performing various physical acts on a customized motorcycle that was lowered from the ceiling. I had read about the show in several American publications, and having authored a book on the subject of motorcycles and their relation to sex, felt a research visit for *Motorcycle Sex*, 2nd edition, was deserved.

The show was interesting, more for the reactions of an American yuppie couple wearing Harley-Davidson T-shirts than the faked acts of passion from the performers. The bikers' negativity was more due to the

This Russian motorcyclist saw me pull into a gas station and turned around to meet me. He spoke no English but took me to a friend who did. I later learned that he had built his Honda over one winter from smuggled parts out of Japan. What he could not find he made by hand. When I told him that it must have been a long, painstaking process, he smiled and said there wasn't much else to do in Siberia in the winter.

German biker artist "Rudi." The painting on the left he titled *Motorcycle* and the one on the right *Ducati*. When not painting in Chiang Mai, Thailand, he can be found riding dirt bikes and dual-sports in the jungles of the Golden Triangle.

walk that was the landmark sign for the club. As he was passing under it, looking up, my friend and I exited. We also were looking up at the motorcycle. On the notorious Patpong Street, famed for its lady shows and working women, Rich and I must have looked very much out of place as we hugged, slapped each other on the back, and laughed at where we were standing.

Business cards with your e-mail address and other information are a timesaving way to keep in touch with friends you make on the road.

fact that the custom motorcycle prop was a Honda than the lack of effort on the part of the performers.

After the show ended, my guest and I walked out the front of the club and almost bowled over Rich. He had been walking down the crowded street when he noticed the motorcycle suspended over the side-

Again we spent a long evening talking about motorcycles, touring routes, and experiences. Knowing that I would be in northern Thailand for Christmas several weeks later with a small group of expatriates and global tourers for a Christmas Day party, I invited Rich to join us if his tour permitted.

In Thailand my "big bike" at 600-cc was about 500 ccs larger than 99 percent of the other motorcycles in the country. When this pretty woman asked me to take her for a ride I knew it was because of the motorcycle. Later she graced the cover of an American motorcycle magazine, with my motorcycle. If she had been able to touch the ground when sitting on the bike I would have had to let her drive it, but she was happy on the back.

Rich said he doubted he could make it because he planned on working his way east into Laos and Cambodia. We parted, again promising to keep in touch, but again our seeing each other seemed unlikely as his tour was coming to an end and he was headed more southerly toward his native Australia than north toward the Golden Triangle.

Christmas Day came and our group was happily eating a large American-style Christmas dinner when in walked Rich. It was a pleasant surprise and our group welcomed him warmly. His motorcycle had needed work before leaving Bangkok, and it had taken him the time since our last meeting to get the needed parts. Once the motorcycle was running he decided to make a visit to our party, an eight-hour ride north, rather than spend Christmas in Buddhist Laos, but he almost killed himself in doing so.

Outside Bangkok he had stopped below the crest of a hill on the road to take a photograph. Rather than park on the left side shoulder of the road, which leaned downwards, he crossed to the right lane and parked. This allowed his heavily loaded touring bike to lean less radically on the side stand because of the upward pitch of the road.

After he took his photograph he returned to his motorcycle and rode off quickly toward the top of the hill, forgetting that in Thailand the traffic drives in the left lane, not in the right. As he reached the top of the hill a small police pick-up truck coming from the opposite direction did too. Rich, trying frantically to avoid a head-on accident, veered left. The policeman in the truck tried the same maneuver.

People are often more curious about my motorcycle and my touring than I am of them.

The result was Rich rode head-on into the truck, flew over his windscreen, and onto the windshield of the police truck. While he knocked himself out, his padded

riding pants and jacket, helmet, boots, and gloves saved him from serious injury. The motorcycle was also only slightly damaged with a dented front wheel. However, the police truck had suffered some front-end damage. After Rich was determined to be roadworthy the police escorted him to the next town where they had the damaged truck inspected for the cost of repairs. Rich forked over $750 and was turned loose to continue his ride to our Christmas Party.

When he walked in he said the reason he had come was to talk with me about the repairs he had made in Bangkok and what I had discovered in Laos. But our group suggested he came because he was an Aussie, and Aussies being cheap tourers, would always sniff out a free meal. Again, Rich and I spent many hours talking and sharing touring tips and experiences. Although I had switched motorcycles to a brand different from his, we were still gear-head brothers and global tourers. Again, when we parted we agreed to keep in touch.

Rich went on to finish his tour of the world and returned to Australia. I sent him a birthday greeting a year later and he wrote back that he had a job, trying to work himself out of debt, part of that being the $750 he was assessed on Christmas Day for $100 worth of repairs to a Thai police truck. Since we were no longer sharing

The Amazonas Motorcycle Club of Brazil adopted me for the afternoon. They were surprised to find that an American would choose to tour Brazil on an Amazonas, their national motorcycle. They wondered why I had not shipped a Harley-Davidson to Brazil to ride. When they discovered my interest in their Amazonas motorcycles, I was warmly welcomed to join them. Sadly, I spoke almost no Portuguese and few of them spoke any English, but we became great friends through our love of motorcycles.

KEEPING IN TOUCH

Business cards with your e-mail address and other information are a timesaving way to keep in touch with friends you make on the road. Handing them a card ensures they can read your name and address later versus you or them hurriedly scribbling the information down on scraps of paper. If they are done specifically for your trip they can give other information such as your motorcycle details, website address, and description of your tour. Mine are closer to 4 x 6 inches, like a file card, with one side blank. I am constantly using the back to write down things like other travelers' addresses and names when they do not have a card, notes to be left on friends' bikes, and maps or directions when I need them. Mine are printed on regular paper, not card stock, for ease of storing in my wallet.

You meet all kinds while touring on a motorcycle. This young woman represents the more youthful end of the spectrum. *Darwin Holmstrom*

information of our touring, I seldom heard from him after he reached home. When he gets ready to make another long tour I look forward to joining him again, trading gearhead stories of our lives on the road, tips on where to find spare parts, and where to make and meet special friends.

MAKING NEW FRIENDS

Riding through Wyoming on Interstate 25 I saw a Triumph motorcycle with a British license plate parked on the shoulder. There was no rider around, only the motorcycle on the center stand. As I rode by at 75 miles per hour I wondered if it had run out of gas and the rider had hitchhiked to town. Or possibly it had broken and the pilot had gone in search of a truck. My next thought was how easily it could be lifted into a passing pick-up truck on the desolate highway and be gone by the time the owner returned. I decided I had enough time to turn around and baby-sit it for a few hours.

As I rode up to it, a rider in a full red leather riding suit stood up from where he had been laying in the tall grass in the ditch below the road surface. I turned off my motorcycle, took off my helmet, and asked him if he was OK. In his British accent he answered that he was and had only been taking a nap in the cool grass. I told him that was where the rattlesnakes like to nap during the day too. He gulped, and then thanked me for the advice, saying in his country they did not have rattlesnakes.

We spent some minutes chatting about where he was from, where he was going, and took photographs of each other. We shared some of our common touring experiences and dislikes, such as riding through India and Nepal.

I then asked if he needed a place to stay for the night and offered a clean bed and a meal in my house three hours farther south. He said he would like a shower and meal, but he had to be in Texas by morning. He asked about a new rear tire because his was nearly bald. It being a Sunday, I told him we could make a few calls and possibly fix him up, but at least could get him a shower and good meal. When I asked him what his hurry was, he told me he was trying to set a record for being the fastest man around the world on a motorcycle.

We rode together into Denver, got him showered and fed, then back on the road several hours later. During our time together we shared information on the road ahead, contact names, and gearhead babble of tires, oils, and motorcycles. In exchange for my help he took the time out of his record-setting ride to teach me how to send and receive e-mail on my computer.

The rider, named Nick, left and eventually set his world record. We exchanged e-mail from time to time, then found our routes again crossing at a motorcycle traveler's meeting in Belgium the following spring. He

told me of a new lady in his life and possible wedding bells in the fall.

Later that year, I was on another tour of the world which routed me through Munich during Intermot, the large international motorcycle show. There I saw Nick again, doing a presentation for Triumph. He offered me half of his dry hotel room for the night instead of me having to camp in the rain. In exchange, I laughingly agreed to put my world tour on hold long enough to reverse directions and ride to London some days later and watch him get married.

Sixteen international riders who had successfully completed one tour of the world. This was taken in Belgium as I was preparing for a third long ride by gathering information at a meeting of global tourers. Author Ted Simon is on the lower right and the "fastest man around the world" on a motorcycle, Nick Sanders, is standing next to me in the middle.

Touring Africa I often met local people who could not speak English and I could not understand their language, but we had a common affection for motorcycles. Here I offered to let one sit on the motorcycle while I took his picture, and before I could get the camera setup the others had jumped in to be included. They were a bunch of happy fellows.

Without a doubt one of most people-pressing places I toured on the planet was through Bangladesh. It was not uncommon to find 50 to 100 people gathering around my motorcycle if I stopped. They were friendly and curious, but often overwhelming. If I wanted to check my oil level or tire pressure I would immediately have a crowd watching, sometimes pushing right up against me.

A year later I had finished my ride around the world and was back home only doing weekend tours while trying to make enough money for another long ride. Nick was leading a group of clients on a ride around the United States, then on to Alaska. Our paths crossed in Colorado and we again spent an enjoyable few hours trading road stories. A look at our calendars and travel routes for the coming month found us both in New York City on the same dates. A plan was made and we later met for an afternoon of touristing, including some photographs of each other on

the top of one of two twin towers that will never be photographed again.

Nick and I still maintain contact, but less so now that our solo global touring has slowed. In his book about setting his world record, he mentions a piece of wisdom I flippantly opined on that windy Wyoming afternoon when we met that has stayed with him. He had asked me what I was looking for while touring on my motorcycle. I answered I was seeking answers about love and life, knowing they were out there on the highways of the world somewhere in the wind. He has since found some answers, I less, but we still remain good friends and share what we have found.

People are often more curious about my motorcycle and my touring than I am of them. When I am touring alone they often approach me, as I am less threatening than if I am riding with someone else or in a group. It is as if I am more vulnerable alone and more easily approached.

At the extreme are places like India and Bangladesh, where a tourer on a motorcycle is a novelty, something not seen before. Light-skinned tourists in tour groups or walking around with backpacks are common, but a motorcyclist, and especially

In Siberia I was invited to spend the night at this dacha outside of Chita. The ladies made me my first home-cooked meal in months and prepared a traditional bath for me to sample. While "Mom" spoke no English and my Russian was limited to less than 100 words, we were able to have a memorable evening and promised to keep in touch, which we have done through third parties.

one wearing clothing not seen before and on a motorcycle larger that 99 percent of all other motorcycles in the country, makes for something very interesting. Sometimes being the center of so much attention is almost oppressive.

In India I had to resort to a whistle to clear people away from my motorcycle whenever I stopped. The traffic police are not issued guns in India. Instead they are given whistles which are judiciously used to get people's attention or to clear them, as the whistle represents authority. To make enough working space to do routine maintenance on my motorcycle I would blow my police-like whistle and the crowd would back away. The people were not being unfriendly, just curious. As one traveler explained, the people were curious about me, curious about the tools, and most curious that I had tools and knew how to use them.

When a child approaches me when I am touring I can almost feel their desire to freely move on two wheels; I lusted after the same at their age.

There is an interest in the motorcycle tourer that is not found in the average tourist. The motorcycle tourer is seen as an individual, someone quite different from the routine traveler, seemingly free to map his or her own courses, take chances and live on the road. To the non-motorcycle tourer, those elements are often something they would like to have had they the money, time, and ability. Instead they do not, but are interested in getting close to those who do in hopes that some of what they don't have will rub off from the traveler who does. That interest has often been expressed to me by people I am sure would not approach me if I were not touring on a motorcycle.

As a touring motorcyclist, people of other motorcycle lifestyles can readily relate to you. Your being on a motorcycle sends a message to them that says, "You and I have

something in common: life on the road riding two wheels." This commonality can quickly make you friends, some that you never dreamed of having.

STURGIS

I once rode my 1960 BMW R69S to the annual Sturgis Rally. Arriving in a pouring rain I rode into a camping field that was filled with Harley-Davidson motorcycles, nearly 10,000 of them. As I struggled to get my tent up in the wind and wet, several other campers came over to help me. After I got it pitched and my things inside I thanked them with an offer to buy them a

Sturgis is great fun for an adult motorcyclist, but not exactly family-friendly. Shown above are the late, great Karl "Big Daddy Rat" and a few of his closest friends. *Darwin Holmstrom*

BEING NOTICED

There is a general fascination with motorcycles around the world. When touring a country where 99 percent of the population will never be able to purchase either a car or a motorcycle, and the 1 percent that can will only be able to afford something in the 50- to 110-cc range, a big bike, anything over 250 cc, is naturally a curiosity. Those that cannot afford a motorcycle often wish only to touch the gas tank or some of the gizmos and gadgets attached. Others are thrilled to have their picture taken merely standing next to a large touring motorcycle.

One of the easiest places on the earth to tour on a motorcycle is America. No matter how far you ride in the lower 48, you are seldom in danger of breaking down and being alone. Restaurants and motels are always within an hour or two of riding.

Cell phones and electronic gizmos make motorcycle touring so easy I often say a blind man could do it. Some scoff at such a suggestion, but agree that if you sat a chimp on top of the right kind of motorcycle and gave it a push start, the chimp could manage a fair distance without falling down or

I stopped on this empty jungle road only long enough to take a photo of the emptiness, but before I could walk 20 feet and take out the camera I found these two children who appeared out of nowhere. They dropped down in the sand and stared at my motorcycle, probably the largest they had ever seen at 500 cc. When I rode off they ran after me yelling and waving. I felt like the movie character Shane.

As hard as I tried I could not get this Masai warrior to smile. He wanted to sit on my motorcycle and I agreed, but only if I could take a photograph. This was the best I could get from him on camera. Off camera he would laugh and smile, but on film he wanted to be as serious as he could be.

riding off the road across Kansas on Interstate 70. So what would prevent a person declared legally blind from wiring themselves up to a GPS, CB, and then riding tandem on the same slab of concrete across Kansas?

One of my weaknesses is children wanting to sit on, ride, or touch my motorcycles. Part of this is due to my having wanted to ride motorcycles when I was young and not being able to do so. When a child approaches me when I am touring I can almost feel their desire to freely move on two wheels. I lusted after the same at their age. If I cannot take them for a ride because there are too many or it would not be safe to do so, then I try to accommodate their pleas to wear my riding gloves. After several run-ins with head lice, however, I have quit letting them try on my motorcycle helmet.

In Africa these children wanted me to take their picture, which I did. The driver begged me to let him wear my motorcycle helmet, which I did. Three days later I discovered the driver had head lice, which I did.

I found this group of "baby monks" in Sikkum at a mountain monastery. They wanted to be photographed with my motorcycle and one wanted to wear my helmet and gloves. Three days later I discovered the little monk had head lice, as did I.

beer later on. They refused, saying they had plenty of beer, but could use the company of a lady if I happened to have one in my saddlebag—they'd also settle for me or some of my BMW friends joining later.

Their implication was clear. Because I was riding a BMW and not a Harley-Davidson I was less than a full man, closer to something with breasts or a girl-boy. I began to worry about what my night was going to develop into after my neighbors had a few more of their beers aplenty.

The rain stopped and two of the Harley riders wandered over to look at my motorcycle. They wanted to know how far I rode that day, and when I told them just under 600 miles, that impressed them. One offered me a beer from a proffered dangling half-empty six-pack. The other asked about the driveshaft on my BMW while inspecting it. While we tipped our cans we talked about how nice it was to have an enclosed driveshaft bathed in oil that never needed attention like a messy set of sprockets and chains.

Over the next two days my new friends shared meals and camaraderie with me, once telling a drunk to stay away from my motorcycle when he tried to sit on it. They were very interested in my stories of touring foreign countries and what the roads, people, food, and beer were like. When we parted I had made some new friends who I looked forward to seeing the next year when I returned. They told me they thought I was OK because I rode a "neat old beemer." Then they added, "If you'd come in here on some Jap crap, we'd have burned it."

I first tried riding a camel in Namibia. After a few minutes on the camel I decided I preferred touring by motorcycle. Not only was the ride uncomfortable, but it was slow, and the smell let out by the camel in front was enough to make me want to start smoking again . . . Camel cigarettes, of course.

CAMELS

There seems to be some foolish belief that if a person can ride a motor-cycle they can "ride" other forms of transport. I was touring Namibia when I stopped to take some photographs of a train of camels. The woman who owned the camels was delighted that I wanted to take pictures of her camels. She considered them her pets, much like our family dog or cat. While I was taking photographs she was asking me questions like where I was from, where I was going, how long I had been on the road, and how I paid for my travels. When I was done with my photographs she asked me if I wanted to try riding one of her camels. I told her I did not think I could, it looked awkward and uncomfortable. She said it would not be more difficult than riding my motorcycle. My ego took over and within minutes I was climbing on a kneeling camel.

As the camel stood up I knew I had made a mistake. Unlike my motorcycle, there were no handlebars to hold onto and no foot pegs to support my feet. I started to slide off before I grabbed something to hold onto, one ear of the camel. That really got the camel's attention and it tried to shake me loose by bucking and snarling. When I let go of the ear the camel turned its head fully around and clamped its teeth on to my leg. That was the end of my first camel ride. I slid off the side of it and crashed hard on the ground, the first crash I experienced while touring Africa. As I stood up and started to check for broken bones the camel spit on me.

Riding in Rajastan, India, I saw a camel market where several hundred of the lump-backed beasts were being offered for sale. I rode my motorcycle into the center and made a deal with an owner to trade a photo-graph of his camel for a ride on the back of my motorcycle. He misunderstood me and soon had me being helped onto his camel for a camel ride. This camel was less frisky than the first one I tried to ride and did not try to bounce me off. Instead it stood very still while the owner took my photo. Once I was off the beast it hacked up a large wad of camel spit on my leg.

Overall, the best motorcycle tours are those you tailor to fit your own needs and goals.

FINAL THOUGHTS

Overall, the best motorcycle tours are those you tailor to fit your own needs and goals. An acquaintance of mine tours by motorcycle nearly every weekend during the summer. His vacation is planned around making a motorcycle tour some-where. But his definition of motorcycle touring and mine are quite different. For him, touring means riding his fully equipped touring motorcycle with his wife following in the pick-up truck. Each night finds them nestled in a nicely appointed motel after enjoying a multicourse dinner at a nearby upscale restaurant. When clouds loom they load the motorcycle in the back of the pickup, cover it with a motorcycle cover, and share the cab until the wet weather stops.

On the same route you will find me, generally riding solo, eating fast food or take-out from the local grocery store, and wondering why there are so many cigarette burns on the nightstand next to my lumpy bed in a cheap motel, or listening to the rain on my tent. When the weekend is over and both my acquaintance and I are home, my scale of motorcycle touring satisfaction dips no further than his. And that is the great thing about motorcycle touring: We can both do it our own way and neither one of us wrong.

My second attempt at touring by camel was this free ride in India. While one camel herder tried to get the camel to move, the other took my picture. This second attempt included wearing my motorcycle helmet and gloves. I had learned from the first camel ride that they could bite and spit. After the free camel ride, the owner wanted to trade me his camel for my motorcycle. We had great fun laughing at him sitting on my motorcycle and me wiping camel spit off my riding pants.

After touring the world four times, and having logged more than 1 million miles, I still don't have all the answers to the tricks of successful touring. I know what has worked for me and always welcome contributions from other touring riders on what may work better or what works for them. If you see me somewhere, stop and share your thoughts. I'll hope to see you out there . . . on the road.

Index

APPENDIX: READING RESOURCES

Adventure Motorcycling Handbook, Chris Scott. A good guide for more extreme tourers looking to ride both on and off-road. Trailblazer Publications, ISBN 1-873756-37-2.

Motorcycle Touring and Travel, Bill Stermer. A beginners guide to touring, targeted to pavement riders in the United States. Whitehorse Press, ISBN 1-884313-15-9.

The Complete Idiot's Guide to Motorcycles, Darwin Holmstrom. The biker's handbook on everything from touring bikes to outlaw gangs and touring clubs. Alpha Publishing, ISBN 0-02-864258-9

Alaska by Motorcycle: How to Motorcycle to Alaska, Dr. Gregory W. Frazier. How to prepare yourself and your motorcycle for the ride to Alaska. Arrowstar Publishing, ISBN 0-935151-47-8

Riding South: Mexico, Central, and South America by Motorcycle, Dr. Gregory W. Frazier. How to prepare and tour the countries of South America. Arrowstar Publishing, ISBN 0-935151-04-4

Europe by Motorcycle, Dr. Gregory W. Frazier. A "how to" book for the motorcyclist thinking about touring Europe. Arrowstar Publishing, ISBN 0-935151-49-4

New Zealand by Motorcycle, Dr. Gregory W. Frazier. The "ins and outs" of touring the land of the kiwis by motorcycle. Arrowstar Publishing, ISBN 0-935151-22-2

Total Control, Lee Parks. How to control your motorcycle, what the other riding-skills books don't tell you. Motorbooks International, ISBN 0-7603-1403-9.

Motorcycle Camping Made Easy, Bob Woofter. A beginner's guide to motorcycle touring while camping. Whitehorse Press, ISBN 1-884313-33-7.

Proficient Motorcycling: The Ultimate Guide to Riding Well. David Hough. An expert's guide to riding well. Bowtie Press, ISBN 1-889540-53-6

Street Strategies, David Hough. How to improve your survival skills in traffic. Bowtie Press, ISBN 1-889540-69-2

Lightweight Unsupported Motorcycle Travel for Terminal Cases, Aero Design and Mfg. Co., Inc. Touring gurus from Motorcycle Touring Central share a wealth of tidbits for the two-wheel traveler. Aero Designs and Mfg. Co., Inc. (www.aerostitch.com)

Route 66 Lost and Found
ISBN 0-7603-1854-9
137232AP

Leanings
ISBN 0-7603-1158-7
134919AP

Leanings 2
ISBN 0-7603-2164-7
139445AP

Total Control
ISBN 0-7603-1403-9
135935AP

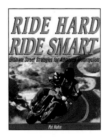

Ride Hard, Ride Smart
ISBN 0-7603-1760-7
137224AP

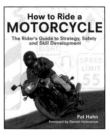

How to Ride a Motorcycle
ISBN 0-7603-2114-0
139309AP

**101 Sportbike
Performance Projects**
ISBN 0-7603-1331-8
135742AP

**101 Harley-Davidson Twin Cam
Performance Projects**
ISBN 0-7603-1639-2
136265AP

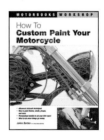

**How to Custom Paint
Your Motorcycle**
ISBN 0-7603-2033-0
138639AP